SELECTED WRITINGS

ARTHUR SYMONS was born in Milford Haven in 1865. He lived in London, where he frequented the Rhymers' Club, a group of writers who met at the Cheshire Cheese in Fleet Street between 1891 and 1894. A friend of Ernest Dowson, Lionel Johnson and Wilde, he was an important influence on Yeats, with whom he shared lodgings for a time. He contributed to *The Yellow Book* and became editor of *The Savoy*. Symons was fluent in French and Italian; his *The Symbolist Movement in Literature* (1899) was influential in introducing French Symbolism to English readers. He was also a translator of Baudelaire and Zola, and a leading literary critic. Symons died in 1945.

ROGER HOLDSWORTH lectures in English at the University of Manchester. He has edited plays by Jonson and Middleton, and has been a General Editor of the Malone Society.

Fyfield*Books* aim to make available some of the great classics of British and European literature in clear, affordable formats, and to restore often neglected writers to their place in literary tradition.

Fyfield*Books* take their name from the Fyfield elm in Matthew Arnold's 'Scholar Gypsy' and 'Thyrsis'. The tree stood not far from the village where the series was originally devised in 1971.

> *Roam on! The light we sought is shining still.*
> *Dost thou ask proof? Our tree yet crowns the hill,*
> *Our Scholar travels yet the loved hill-side*

from 'Thyrsis'

ARTHUR SYMONS

Selected Writings

Edited with an introduction by
ROGER HOLDSWORTH

Fyfield*Books*

CARCANET

I am deeply grateful to Miss Clare Colvin for her constant help and encouragement. I should also like to thank Dr Paul Crossley, Mr Kevin Doyle and Mr Grevel Lindop.

First published in Great Britain in 1974 by
Carcanet Press Limited
Alliance House
Cross Street
Manchester M2 7AQ

This impression 2003
Selection, introduction and editorial matter © Roger Holdsworth
1974, 1989, 2003

A CIP catalogue record for this book is available from the British Library
ISBN 1 85754 726 8

The publisher acknowledges financial assistance from Arts Council England

Printed and bound in England by SRP Ltd, Exeter

CONTENTS

5

7

PROSE

Introduction

INTEREST in the poetry of the 1890s has grown steadily during the present century. Desmond Flower's edition of Ernest Dowson appeared in 1934, Ian Fletcher's of Lionel Johnson in 1953. Four years later Frank Kermode's *Romantic Image* illuminated the period as a vitally organic phase in a developing poetic tradition, and since then we have come to view the poetry and criticism of the 'nineties as not only intrinsically worthy of serious study, but as important for its profound influence on that literature of our own time which we regard as most typically 'modern'. In spite of this Arthur Symons, in many ways a key figure, has remained out of print for over forty years.

Such neglect is the more surprising when one considers that the three major poets of the first half of this century – Yeats, Pound, and Eliot – all stressed their debt to Symons as the critic who introduced them to the French symbolists, writers whose work was to have a crucial formative effect on their own. For Yeats the introduction came in the early 1890s, when Symons began making regular trips to Paris, bringing back enthusiastic reports to his fellow Rhymers (among them Yeats) of the writers he met there, and translating their work. In 1893 he was able to arrange Verlaine's celebrated visit to England, as well as to publish 'The Decadent Movement in Literature', the survey which established him as the leading interpreter of literary trends on the continent. In his *Memoirs* Yeats records that Symons 'desired a little too obviously to speak with all famous, interesting men', but his remarks in *Auto-biographies* show a keen awareness of the benefits that all this activity brought:

Arthur Symons, more than any man I have ever known, could slip as it were into the mind of another, and my thoughts gained in richness and in clearness from his sympathy, nor shall I ever know how much my practice and my theory owe to the passages that he read me from Catullus and from Verlaine and Mallarmé. . . . He was making those translations from Mallarmé and from Verlaine, from Caldéron, from Saint John of the Cross, which are the most accomplished metrical translations of our time, and I think that those from Mallarmé may have given elaborate form to my verses of those years, to the latter poems of *The Wind Among the Reeds*, to *The Shadowy Waters*.

Symons anticipated these compliments by dedicating to Yeats *The Symbolist Movement in Literature* (1899), and by citing him in the preface as 'the chief representative of that movement in our country'. 'Symbolism' now replaces 'decadence', though largely because the latter term has been redefined. In the earlier essay it had described 'the most representative literature of the day', a literature charac- terised by 'an intense self-consciousness' and by 'a restless curiosity in research'. Now 'decadence' is restricted solely to style, to 'that ingenious deformation of the language, in Mallarmé for instance', while 'symbolism', though it embraces the same group of writers and takes in others, is used to make a much larger claim for their work: 'It is all an attempt to spiritualise literature, to evade the old bondage of rhetoric, the old bondage of exteriority . . . to disengage the ultimate essence, the soul, of whatever exists and can be realised by the consciousness.' The book proved tremendously influential. It familiarised contemporary English readers with the European movement and fostered a spirit of internationalism in literature which is still with us. It was closely studied by the Imagists and by Eliot. Pound, for example, wrote to René Taupin in May 1928:

Influence fr. sur moi – relativement tard. Rapports fr. < eng. via Arthur Symons etc. 1908. Baudelaire, Verlaine etc. . . . l'idée de l'image doit 'quelque chose' aux symbolistes français via T. E. Hulme, via Yeat[s] < Symons < Mallarmé. Comme le pain doit quelque chose au vanneur de blé.

And in *The Sacred Wood* Eliot celebrated *The Symbolist Movement* as 'an introduction to wholly new feelings . . . a revelation'. Else- where he gave a more detailed account:

I myself owe Mr Symons a great debt; but for having read his book I should not, in the year 1908, have heard of Laforgue or Rimbaud; I should probably not have begun to read Verlaine; and but for reading Verlaine, I should not have heard of Corbière. So the Symons book is one of those which have affected the course of my life.*

'English poetry and criticism', Professor Kermode observes in his chapter on Symons in *Romantic Image*, 'have been changed by his book . . . and that is as much as a critic can achieve'.

But it was not only with his criticism that Symons helped to shape the character of modern poetry. As a poet he was vividly conscious that his age was 'an age without convictions', that the pressure of an increasingly scientific, materialist, urban culture was altering the nature of contemporary experience, that the artist was losing his sense of an audience. It was an age which made special demands of the poet; he must select different material and treat it in a different way. 'To be modern in poetry, to represent really oneself and one's surroundings, the world as it is today, to be modern and yet poetical, is, perhaps, the most difficult, as it is certainly the most interesting, of all artistic achievements.' The city, Symons concluded in the same essay ('Modernity in Verse', 1892), held the key to this achievement: 'I think that might be the test of poetry which professes to be modern: its capacity for dealing with London, with what one sees or might see there, indoors or out', and many of his poems, particularly in *Days and Nights*, *Silhouettes*, and *London Nights*, can be seen as an attempt to 'represent really', and to anatomise, the complex, 'artificial' character of city life.

It is true that the methods employed seem at first inadequate for the task in hand. Yeats notes in *Autobiographies* that Lionel Johnson was especially unimpressed:

Arthur Symons' poetry made him angry, because it would substitute for that achievement [of the intellect] Parisian impressionism, 'a London fog, the blurred tawny lamplight, the red omnibus, the dreary rain, the depressing mud, the glaring gin-shop, the slatternly shivering women, three dexterous stanzas telling you that and nothing more'.

Symons, always an ardent believer in the fundamental identity of the arts, had founded many key elements of his style on that of Whistler,

* Review of Peter Quennell's *Baudelaire and the French Symbolists* in *The Criterion*, ix (1930), no. 35, p. 357.

Degas, and the French Impressionist painters, and in consequence the reader is regularly presented (as in 'Pastel: Masks and Faces') simply with an 'image', a series of fleeting subjective impressions which deftly sketch a scene and evoke a mood, but do not seek to impose – at least not explicitly – any social or moral interpretations. Nor is there any attempt to provide the panoramic perspective of, for example, Whitman, a poet whom Symons hailed as the creator of 'a vital poetry of cities' even while he deplored his sprawling formlessness and the hectoring vulgarity of his style. (An American poet can be cited here, however: Poe, whose dictum 'a long poem is a paradox' Symons fully approved.) Johnson's strictures are none the less misplaced. It is precisely Symons's ability to focus sharply on the telling detail, to capture the essential flavour of a scene with swift, sure strokes – to fetch out, in fact, 'the images which hurt and connect' – which enables him to create in the reader a sense that each briefly glimpsed scene is part of a wider, unseen context – the context of the city. As a recent critic has observed:

Symons' imagistic exercises are genuinely innovative . . . . He becomes increasingly able to give the scattered facts of the city a metaphoric significance, and is, in fact, the first English poet who was able to write about London with something like Baudelaire's mythographic sense, to make the city a convincing milieu of spiritual adventures. The poet progresses from an assembling of the diverse images of city life to poetic situations which are modified or even created by the ambient city.*

The progress can be traced from an early poem like 'The Street-Singer' through 'In the Haymarket' (which strikingly anticipates the style of Hardy's *Satires of Circumstance*), to the fully matured technique displayed in 'White Heliotrope' and '*La Mélinite: Moulin Rouge*', the study of Jane Avril which Yeats admired as 'one of the most perfect lyrics of our time'.

Symons's attention to the sexual underworld of the city, to prostitutes and their clients, 'Juliets of a night', 'the chance romances of the streets', this too was a new departure. Prostitution had long been an unavoidable fact of life in Victorian London (in the 1860s

* G. R. Stange, 'The Frightened Poets', in *The Victorian City: Images and Realities*, ed. H. J. Dyos and M. Wolff, 2 vols., 1973, p. 491.

Hippolyte Taine had reported that in the Haymarket and the Strand 'every hundred steps one jostles twenty harlots'), but hitherto no poet had attempted such scenes as the following:

> The little bedroom papered red,
> The gas's faint malodorous light,
> And one beside me in the bed,
> Who chatters, chatters, half the night . . . ('Leves Amores')

> As I lay on the stranger's bed,
> And clasped the stranger-woman I had hired,
> Desiring only memory dead
> Of all that I had once desired . . . ('To One in Alienation')

So too with the imagery which accompanies this theme: cigarettes, maquillage, tumbled beds and scented boudoirs, none had appeared in English poetry before.

Eliot, of course, is the English poet with whom we most readily associate this mythographic sense of the city, yet on several occasions he may have relied on Symons, perhaps unconsciously, for his ideas. I have in mind not Symons's poetry – though this too, as we shall see below, may be in question – but his impressionist prose piece *London: A Book of Aspects* (1909). Here as in *The Waste Land* one finds a landscape of despair, a nightmarish vision of a London which is 'the wreck and moral of civilisation'. Its inhabitants are 'like prisoners'; there is 'something inevitably automatic' in their behaviour; their lives are blighted by 'soiled sordid ostentation' and by 'the pompous and distressing unrealities of a great city'. In *The Waste Land* one finds not only the typist smoothing her hair 'with automatic hand', but the same enveloping sense of unreality:

> Unreal City,
> Under the brown fog of a winter dawn,
> A crowd flowed over London Bridge, so many,
> I had not thought death had undone so many.

In these lines, as Eliot points out in the Notes, postwar London merges into Dante's Limbo in the *Inferno*; yet this too is echoed in Symons's book:

13

There is nothing in the world quite like a London fog, though. . . . Dante has described it in the 'Inferno' when he speaks of the banks of a pit in hell, 'crusted over with a mould from the vapour below, which cakes upon them, and battles with eye and nose'.

Elsewhere other poems by Eliot are called to mind: 'Prufrock', for example, by the way that Symons credits London fog with an independent, animal existence, and views it as a kind of objective correlative of physical and mental torpor:

It is as if one tried the experience of drowning or suffocating. . . . It stifles the mind as well as choking the body. It comes on slowly and stealthily, picking its way, choosing its direction, leaving contemptuous gaps in its course; then it settles down like a blanket of solid smoke, which you can feel but not put from you.

And consider, finally, the following passage; besides anticipating the opening of 'Rhapsody on a Windy Night', it summarises many of the themes of Eliot's poetry up to 1922:

As I passed through the Saturday night crowd lately, between two opposing currents of evil smells, I overheard a man who was lurching along the pavement say in contemptuous comment: 'Twelve o'clock! we may all be dead by twelve o'clock!' He seemed to sum up the philosophy of that crowd, its listlessness, its hard unconcern, its failure to be interested. Nothing matters, he seemed to say for them, let us drag out our time until the time is over, and the sooner it is over the better.

Life in great cities dishumanises humanity; it envelops the rich in multitudes of clogging costly trifles, and cakes the poor about with ignoble dirt and the cares of unfruitful labour.

Eliot's view of London is, admittedly, more profound. Symons's *London* remains 'a book of aspects', while the layers of association in *The Waste Land* constantly open much wider perspectives, both in time and space; and Eliot, unlike Symons, never hankers sentimentally after a never-never land of pastoral innocence and tranquillity. The parallels suggest, nevertheless, a remarkable sympathy of vision.

Symons's poetic style, in its lucidity and direct, colloquial tone, also reflects his desire 'to be modern in poetry'. Simplicity of style was, he saw, indispensable, and he was quick to realise that this was an essential strength of Yeats's early verse. In a perceptive essay in *Studies on Prose and Verse* (1904) he praises Yeats for his 'rejection of every artifice', his 'return to the natural chant out of which verse was evolved'. He saw too that poetry could not afford to ignore the rhythms of ordinary speech. Browning served as a useful model here (Symons declared his verse 'the most natural, the most vocal . . . of any modern poet'), but his search for a sense of the spoken language led him back also to Donne and to the Elizabethan and Caroline lyric. In 1899, long before Eliot 'discovered' the Metaphysical poets, Symons wrote a sensitive essay on Donne, censuring his 'too knotted thought', but admiring his 'exalted simplicity', his 'forcible, characteristically prosaic' images, and his ability to let the senses 'speak with unparalleled directness'. But even without this essay Symon's debt to the seventeenth-century poets would be obvious, for echoes of them are plentiful in his work. 'Variations upon Love', for example, is consciously derivative:

> For God's sake, let me love you, and give over
> These tedious protestations of a lover;
> We're of one mind to love, and there's no let;
> Remember that, and all the rest forget;
> And let's be happy, mistress, while we may,
> Ere yet tomorrow shall be called today.
> Tomorrow may be heedless, idle-hearted:
> One night's enough for love to have met and parted.
> Then be it now, and I'll not say that I
> In many several deaths for you would die;
> And I'll not ask you to declare that you
> Will longer love than women mostly do.
> Leave words to them whom words, not doings, move,
> And let our silence answer for our love.

The thefts from Donne, Jonson, Marvell, and Crashaw do not need rehearsing. Further evidence of this influence, in poems less like formal exercises, can be traced in 'Clair de Lune', the second stanza of which elaborates Mariana's song in *Measure for Measure*, in 'Song', which imitates Suckling, Carew, and Herrick, and in the quasi-Elizabethan 'Time and Beauty', where an elegant manner is poignantly balanced against strong feeling.

15

The significance of Symons's experiments was not lost on Pound and Eliot. The former wrote to Floyd Dell in 1911: 'I find my sanity in Plato, Dante, Spinoza, Pater, Symons, Longinus. . . . The whole set of "the Rhymers" did valuable work in knocking bombast, & rhetoric & Victorian syrup out of our verse.'* Eliot's comments are more positive (and more sober). In 1957, in a radio programme commemorating the centenary of the birth of Symons's fellow Rhymer, John Davidson, he remarked:

I read John Davidson's poems . . . at a time when I was reading the poets of the 'nineties, who were the only poets – most of them were dead, of course – who at that period of history seemed to have anything to offer to me as a beginner. What I wanted, I think, from the poets of the 'nineties was what they did not have in common with the Pre-Raphaelites, but what was new and original in their work. And I remember three poets in particular. One was Arthur Symons, some of his poems; another was Ernest Dowson, again one or two poems; and the third was Davidson, in his 'Thirty Bob a Week'. From these men I got the idea that one could write poetry in an English such as one would speak oneself. A colloquial idiom. There was a spoken rhythm in some of their poems. . . . And with some of those by the other men I have mentioned, I think it ["Thirty Bob a Week"] prepared me for an initiation into the work of some of the French symbolists, such as Laforgue, whom I came across shortly after.†

It is of course impossible to ascertain which 'one or two poems' by Symons Eliot found so valuable, but one of them may well have been 'Scènes de la Vie de Bohème: *Episode of a Night of May*', written when Symons was only twenty-three. Its theme – *ennui* and the deadening triviality of polite society – is suggestive, as is its studied, ironic casualness of manner. Ian Fletcher has this to say:

The shrug in the voice 'the smiles/Grew chilly, as the best spring evenings do', the confidence of tone, the suggestion of nuances, the ease of topical references, all suggest the 'new' poetry of 20 years later. [*Scènes de la*] *Vie de Bohème* stands half-way between Browning

* G. T. Tanselle, 'Two Early Letters of Ezra Pound', *American Literature*, xxxiv (1962), p. 118.
† Maurice Lindsay, ed., *John Davidson: A Selection of his Poems*, 1961, pp. 8–9.

and Eliot, and like the early Eliot owes something to Laforgue's
Complaintes (1886).*

The similarities can best be illustrated by a comparison of the
following passages:

> He found a chair, Veuve Clicquot, some cigars.
> They emptied glasses and admired the stars,
> The lanterns, night, the sea;
>
> Nature, the newest opera, the dog
> (So clever) who could shoulder arms and dance;
> He mentioned Alphonse Daudet's last romance,
> Last Sunday's river-fog,
>
> Love, Immortality . . .   (*'Episode'*)
>
> Let us take the air, in a tobacco trance,
> Admire the monuments,
> Discuss the late events,
> Correct our watches by the public clocks.
> Then sit for half an hour and drink our bocks.
>   ('Portrait of a Lady')

Other poems yield closer, verbal or metrical parallels. Eliot's

> Eyes that I last saw in tears

for example, recalls both

> Eyes that are not mine to keep
> In the mirror of mine eyes   ('Clair de Lune')

and

> O hands that I have held in mine,
> That knew my kisses and my tears   ('Tears')

while the pattern of sound, the see-sawing rhythm, and the pointed
irony of

* 'Explorations and Recoveries, 2. Symons, Yeats, and the Demonic
Dance', *London Magazine*, vii (1960), no. 6, p. 50.

> Two and two, to and fro,
> They dance to the strains of *Manolo*
>
> ('Scènes de la Vie de Bohème: *At the Ball*')

are very like those of the well-known couplet in 'Prufrock':

> In the room the women come and go
> Talking of Michelangelo.

Symons's impressionist technique may also have influenced Eliot.
Compare

> The feverish room and that white bed,
> The tumbled skirts upon a chair,
> The novel flung half-open, where
> Hat, hair-pins, puffs, and paints are spread
>
> ('White Heliotrope')

with

> Out of the window perilously spread
> Her drying combinations touched by the sun's last rays,
> On the divan are piled (at night her bed)
> Stockings, slippers, camisoles, and stays.
>
> (*The Waste Land*)

'The pictorial arrangement', R. K. R. Thornton notes, 'the
eighteenth-century ability to let juxtaposition do the commenting,
the impersonality', these are common to both passages.* Finally,
one may add that Hardy, too, may have learnt something from
Symons (the two men knew one another well). It is at least very
probable that the famous opening line of 'The Voice'

> Woman much missed, how you call to me, call to me

was supplied by

> Women, much loved, and always mine,
> I call to you across the years

in Symons's 'Tears'.

* ed., *Poetry of the 'Nineties*, 1970, p. 30.

18

All this is not to suggest that Symons was not thoroughly of his time, thoroughly the 'nineties aesthete. On the contrary, it is likely that he both practised and expounded the ideals of the Decadence more energetically than any of his contemporaries. He was fully committed to the fundamental doctrine of *l'Art pour l'Art*, formulated by Gautier in *Mademoiselle de Maupin* (1835) and seconded by Poe in 'The Poetic Principle' (1850); and just as Poe had laid down in 'The Philosophy of Composition' (1846) that 'Beauty is the sole legitimate province of the poem', so Symons asserted in *Plays, Acting, and Music*: 'Art is the creation of beauty in form, visible or audible, and the artist is the creator of beauty in visible or audible form . . . . Art has to do only with the creation of beauty.' Symons was able to appeal to the logical concomitant of this view – the notion that art is free to treat any subject it finds congenial, and is essentially independent of any social or moral function (Poe's 'heresy of the Didactic') – in a rejoinder to the many reviewers who had slated *London Nights* as morbid and pornographic. He wrote in the preface to the second edition:

I have been attacked . . . on the ground of morality, and by people who, in condemning my book, not because it is bad art, but because they think it is bad morality, forget that they are confusing moral and artistic judgements, and limiting art without aiding morality. I contend on behalf of the liberty of art, and I deny that morals may have any right of jurisdiction over it. Art may be served by morality, it can never be its servant.

This was a standard Decadent war-cry. Yeats had echoed it when reviewing *London Nights* ('Mr Symons . . . is less of a savant, or a philosopher, or a moralist, or an historian, than any poet of his time'); Whistler had been shouting it for many years: 'Art should be independent of all clap-trap – should stand alone, and appeal to the artistic sense of eye or ear, without confounding this with emotions entirely foreign to it, as devotion, pity, love, patriotism, and the like.'*

Symons's view of the artist was equally orthodox. His idea, which explains his interest in such 'mad' poets as Cowper, Smart, Clare, Blake, and Poe, that 'the man of genius is fundamentally

* *The Gentle Art of Making Enemies*, 1890, p. 127.

19

abnormal' was typically Decadent, as was his notion that the artist is an isolated seer, wrapped 'in his dream of himself'. Hence his position in *The Symbolist Movement*:

. . . religion, passion, art. . . . Each is a kind of sublime selfishness, the saint, the lover and the artist having each an incommunicable ecstasy which he esteems as his ultimate attainment, however, in his lower moments, he may serve God in action, or do the will of his mistress, or minister to men by showing them a little beauty.

In this view, the artist's life should itself be a work of art; for art becomes 'a kind of religion, with all the duties and responsibilities of the sacred ritual'.

Symons strove to live these ideals. His sense of ritual is amusingly attested by Yeats, describing in his *Memoirs* the two poets' visit to Tulira Castle in Ireland in 1896:

The many rookeries, the square old tower, and the great yard where medieval soldiers had exercised touched our sense of romance. Symons lectured me on my bad manners because, when Martyn showed us two rooms and said we were to choose, I proposed tossing a halfpenny. The place he thought, I suppose, should move one to ceremony.

Similarly, Symons could claim towards the end of his life (despite having been happily married for many years) 'Always . . . I have lived as a solitary soul lives in the midst of the world', and his view that the artist should be both restless and rootless he demonstrated by making frequent extended trips abroad. Yeats was not impressed by this view either, however, as the following illuminating anecdote makes clear. The author is Beerbohm, and the occasion the dinner held to celebrate the publication of the first number of *The Savoy*, edited by Symons, in January 1896. The publisher's wife was officiating:

She did the honours. She dropped little remarks. Yeats was speaking to Aubrey Beardsley whom he met now for the first time, in deep vibrant tones across the table, of the lores and rites of Diabolism – 'Dyahbolism' he called it, thereby making it sound the more fearful. At the other end of the table, Arthur Symons was talking of some foreign city, carrying in his waistcoat-pocket, as it were, the *genius loci*, anon to be embalmed in Pateresque prose. I forget whether this time it was Rome, or Seville, or Moscow or what; but I remember that the hostess said she had never been there. I liked Symons feigning some surprise at this, and for saying that she really ought to go. Presently I heard him saying he thought the nomadic life was the best of all lives for an artist. Yeats, in a pause of his own music, heard this too, and seemed a little pained by it. Shaking back the lock from his brow, he turned to Symons and declared that an artist worked best among his own folk and in the land of his fathers. Symons was rather daunted, but he stuck to his point. He argued that new sights and sounds and odours braced the whole intelligence of a man and quickened his powers of creation. Yeats, gently but firmly, would have none of this. His own arguments may not have been better than Symons'; but, in voice and manner and countenance, Symons was no match for him at all. And it was with a humane impulse that the hostess interposed. 'Mr Symons,' she said, 'is like myself. He likes a little change.' This bathos was so sharp that it was like an actual and visible chasm: one could have sworn to a glimpse of Symons' heels, a faint cry, a thud. Yeats stood for an instant on the brink, stroking his chin enigmatically, and then turned to resume the dropped thread of Dyahbolism.*

Finally, one must note that Symons's own career illustrates all too vividly his belief in the abnormality of the artist. In Italy in the autumn of 1908 he suffered a complete mental breakdown, and was certified insane on 2 November. The diagnosis, general paralysis, was probably incorrect, since Symons made a partial recovery and lived a further thirty-seven years. His biographer argues in favour of manic-depressive psychosis.

Symons's poetry also meets all the requirements of Decadence. Certainly the appeal of his best poems – 'At Dieppe', 'Pastel', 'Impression', 'Javanese Dancers', 'Autumn Twilight', 'Colour Studies', 'White Heliotrope', 'The Andante of Snakes' – is aptly defined by his own definition of Verlaine's poetry in 'The Decadent Movement':

It is the poetry of sensation, of evocation; poetry which paints as well as sings, and which paints as Whistler paints, seeming to think the colours and outlines upon the canvas, to think them only, and they are there. . . . To fix the last fine shade, the quintessence of things; to fix it fleetingly; to be disembodied voice, and yet the voice of a human soul: that is the ideal of Decadence, and it is what Paul Verlaine has achieved.

* R. Lhombreaud, *Arthur Symons: A Critical Biography*, 1963, p. 127.

A poetry, in other words, of suggestion rather than of statement, of nuances rather than of sharp edges; a poetry which specialises, as Symons said of Whistler's painting, in 'moments of faint colour'.

There are further respects in which Symons's poetry may be compared with Verlaine's: in its often languid, melancholy wistfulness, and, more important, in its musicality. Music for the artists of the Decadence represented the ideal of art: the perfect identity of form and content. Verlaine had insisted 'De la musique avant toute chose', Poe had claimed 'It is in Music, perhaps, that the soul most nearly attains . . . the creation of supernal Beauty', and Pater had formulated his famous axiom in 'The School of Giorgione' that 'all art constantly aspires towards the condition of music'. Symons faithfully reflected this preoccupation:

> Music, soft throbbing music in the night,
> Her memory swims
> Into the brain, a carol of delight
> ('Music and Memory')

> Her perfect body, Earth's most eloquent
> Music, the divine human harmony ('Idealism')

> The music had the heat of blood,
> A passion that no words can reach
> ('During Music')

'Words can convey facts', Symons complains in 'Fact in Literature', whereas 'music cannot convey facts at all'; and to the poet this was a problem, for – as Pater had implied by declaring that 'all art does but consist in the removal of surplusage' – every artist must aim at the eradication of discursive content. Thus, the highest praise Symons can offer of Yeats's early verse is that it is 'a mere breathing, in which individual words almost disappear into music'.

If Symons merely reflected this idea, he helped to shape another: that of the dancer, which gradually replaced music as the emblem of the perfect work of art. The dance had for some time fascinated French artists, of course, notably Lautrec, Degas, and Mallarmé, who saw it as 'l'incorporation visuelle de l'idée', and it was to become of crucial importance to Yeats; but in England it was

Symons who first developed the dance as a complex, comprehensive symbol. The subject needs no discussion here (except to note that Yeats called Symons 'a scholar in music-halls as another man might be a Greek scholar or an authority on the age of Chaucer'). It has been brilliantly documented by Professor Kermode in 'Poet and Dancer before Diaghilev', and the many poems on dancing in this selection, plus 'The World as Ballet', which Professor Kermode describes as 'the fullest treatment I know of what may be called the *topos* of the Dancer', speak for themselves.

In some ways, it is true, Symons is decadent rather than Decadent. He is often derivative: '*By the Pool at the Third Rosses*' is pure early Yeats, 'The Last Memory' relies heavily on Yeats's 'When You Are Old', and elsewhere one finds phrases, lines, and cadences stolen more or less unmodified from Browning, Tennyson, and Swinburne. Worse, his revolt against Victorian prudishness occasionally traps him into a strident celebration of vice *pour épater le bourgeois*, and here we might concur with Eliot in *For Lancelot Andrewes*, where he ridicules the 'nineties belief in a 'liturgy of sin' and comments ironically on Symons's propensity to rhyme 'fashions' with 'passions':

Mr Symons seems to us like a sensitive child, who has been taken into a church, and has been entranced with the effigies, and the candles, and the incense. *Such rugs and jugs and candle lights!* . . . For Swinburne's disciples, the men of the 'nineties, Evil was very good fun.

The fevered eroticism, usually spent in more senses than one, is equally unfortunate. It tends to collapse into theatrical absurdity, as in 'Morbidezza', to provoke a complete breakdown of syntax, as in the first stanza of 'Bianca: *Presages*', or, as in the first six lines of '*Moonrise*', to be simply appallingly dull. Again, some of the impressionist poems, for all the poet's curiosity in sensations, remain a random catalogue of superficial 'aspects' (the acuteness of Wilde's assessment of Symons, 'a sad example of an egoist who has no ego', is evident here), and others, such as 'Amoris Exsul: *Twilight*', protest too much that they are colourful. Finally, while admitting the technical virtuosity of 'Nora on the Pavement', with its internal rhyming pattern in the second and fourth lines of each stanza, one must admit also that Symons's more elaborate rhyme schemes can sometimes produce intolerable bathos (the worst example is the final stanza of 'The Armenian Dancer').

But the flaws are not as frequent or as damaging as this tale of woe suggests; nor do they impair one's sense of a poet seeking to organise his vision of the world and experimenting originally with ways of expressing it. As critic, poet, and translator, Symons has both abundance and variety. Wilde even suggested calling him 'Symons Ltd.', adding 'I think one might risk some shares in Symons'. The investment is not unprofitable.

FURTHER READING

The following may be useful in pursuing some of the ideas in the Introduction:

Baugh, E. *A Critical Study of the Writings of Arthur Symons*, University of Manchester Ph.D. thesis, 1964

Ellmann, R. 'Discovering Symbolism', *Golden Codgers*, 1973

Fletcher, I. 'Explorations and Recoveries, 2. Symons, Yeats, and the Demonic Dance', *London Magazine*, vii (1960), no. 6, pp. 46–60

Gordon, Jan B. 'The Danse Macabre of Arthur Symons' *London Nights*', *Victorian Poetry*, ix (1971), pp. 429–43

Kermode, F. *Romantic Image*, 1957

Kermode, F. 'Poet and Dancer before Diaghilev', *Puzzles and Epiphanies*, 1962

Lhombreaud, R. *Arthur Symons: A Critical Biography*, 1963

Munro, J. 'Arthur Symons as Poet: Theory and Practice', *English Literature in Transition*, vi (1963), pp. 212–22

Munro, J. ' "The Symphony of Snakes" and the Development of the Romantic Image', *English Literature in Transition*, vii (1964), pp. 143–5

Stange, G. R. 'The Frightened Poets', *The Victorian City: Images and Realities*, ed. H. J. Dyos and M. Wolff, 2 vols., 1973, ii, pp. 475–94

Temple, Ruth Z. *The Critic's Alchemy: A Study of the Introduction of French Symbolism into England*, New York, 1953

Thornton, R. K. R. ed. *Poetry of the 'Nineties*, 1970

Yeats, W. B. *Autobiographies*, 1955

Yeats, W. B. *Memoirs*, ed. D. Donoghue, 1972

NOTE ON THE TEXT

At the risk of losing some of the 'period' flavour of Symons's 'nineties style, I have based my text of the poems on the revised text of *The Collected Works of Arthur Symons*, 9 vols., 1924, i–iii. The revisions are not, however, extensive, many of them had appeared much earlier in *Poems*, 2 vols., 1902, and they tend in any case to be genuine improvements. A simple example is 'Javanese Dancers', 1.9, where 'glide' replaces 'step'. Another, more complex, is the final stanza of the same poem. Here the Keatsian echoes of

> The little amber-coloured dancers move,
>   Like little painted figures on a screen,
>   Or phantom-dancers haply seen
> Among the shadows of a magic grove

are toned down in the substituted

> In measure while the gnats of music whirr,
>   The little amber-coloured dancers move,
>   Like painted idols seen to stir
> By the idolators in a magic grove

– though it is fair to note a new debt here, to Pope ('Still round and round the ghosts of beauty glide'), perhaps prompted by the earlier revision of 'step'.

Dates and dedications, added to many poems in *The Collected Works*, have been omitted, and the following errors rectified:

'Episode of a Night May', 1.16: sea.] sea;
'Hallucination', 1.39: Or] As
'Song', 1.10: dissemble.] dissemble,
'Isolation', 1.6: cold] old

The textual sources of the translations and prose passages are given at the end of each piece. Dates of first publication are given in the table of contents.

Poetry

From *Days and Nights*

The Fisher's Widow

The boats go out and the boats come in
Under the wintry sky;
And the rain and foam are white in the wind,
And the white gulls cry.

She sees the sea when the wind is wild
Swept by the windy rain;
And her heart's a-weary of sea and land
As the long days wane.

She sees the torn sails fly in the foam,
Broad on the skyline grey;
And the boats go out and the boats come in,
But there's one away.

Scènes de la Vie de Bohème
Episode of a Night of May

The coloured lanterns lit the trees, the grass,
The little tables underneath the trees,
And the rays dappled like a delicate breeze
Each wine-illumined glass.

The pink light flickered, and a shadow ran
Along the ground as couples came and went;
The waltzing fiddles sounded from the tent,
And *Giroflée* began.

They sauntered arm in arm, these two; the smiles
Grew chilly, as the best spring evenings do.
The words were warmer, but the words came few,
And pauses fell at whiles.

But she yawned prettily. 'Come then,' said he.
He found a chair, Veuve Clicquot, some cigars.
They emptied glasses and admired the stars,
The lanterns, night, the sea;

Nature, the newest opera, the dog
(So clever) who could shoulder arms and dance;
He mentioned Alphonse Daudet's last romance,
Last Sunday's river-fog,

Love, Immortality; the talk ran down
To these mere lees: they wearied each of each,
And tortured ennui into hollow speech,
And yawned, to hide a frown.

She jarred his nerves; he bored her – and so soon.
Both were polite, and neither cared to say
The word that mars a perfect night of May.
They watched the waning moon.

The Street-Singer

She sings a pious ballad wearily;
Her shivering body creeps on painful feet
Along the muddy runlets of the street;
The damp is in her throat: she coughs to free
The cracked and husky notes that tear her chest;
From side to side she looks with eyes that grope
Feverishly hungering in a hopeless hope,
For pence that will not come; and pence mean rest,
The rest that pain may steal at night from sleep,
The rest that hunger gives when satisfied;

Her fingers twitch to handle them; she sings
Shriller; her eyes, too hot with tears to weep,
Fasten upon a window, where, inside,
A sweet voice mocks her with its carollings.

The Opium-Smoker

I am engulfed, and drown deliciously.
Soft music like a perfume, and sweet light
Golden with audible odours exquisite,
Swathe me with cerements for eternity.
Time is no more. I pause and yet I flee.
A million ages wrap me round with night.
I drain a million ages of delight.
I hold the future in my memory.

Also I have this garret which I rent,
This bed of straw, and this that was a chair,
This worn-out body like a tattered tent,
This crust, of which the rats have eaten part,
This pipe of opium; rage, remorse, despair;
This soul at pawn and this delirious heart.

From *Silhouettes*

At Dieppe
After Sunset

The sea lies quieted beneath
The after-sunset flush
That leaves upon the heaped grey clouds
The grape's faint purple blush.

Pale, from a little space in heaven
Of delicate ivory,
The sickle-moon and one gold star
Look down upon the sea.

On the Beach

Night, a grey sky, a ghostly sea,
The soft beginning of the rain;
Black on the horizon, sails that wane
Into the distance mistily.

The tide is rising, I can hear
The soft roar broadening far along;
It cries and murmurs in my ear
A sleepy old forgotten song.

Softly the stealthy night descends,
The black sails fade into the sky:
Is not this, where the sea-line ends,
The shore-line of infinity?

I cannot think or dream; the grey
Unending waste of sea and night,
Dull, impotently infinite,
Blots out the very hope of day.

Requies

O is it death or life
That sounds like something strangely known
In this subsiding out of strife,
This slow sea-monotone?

A sound, scarce heard through sleep,
Murmurous as the August bees
That fill the forest hollows deep
About the roots of trees.

O is it life or death,
O is it hope or memory,
That quiets all things with this breath
Of the eternal sea?

Pastel: Masks and Faces

The light of our cigarettes
Went and came in the gloom:
It was dark in the little room.

Dark, and then, in the dark,
Sudden, a flash, a glow,
And a hand and a ring I know.

And then, through the dark, a flush
Ruddy and vague, the grace
(A rose!) of her lyric face.

Morbidezza

White girl, your flesh is lilies,
Under a frozen moon,
So still is
The rapture of your swoon
Of whiteness, snow or lilies.

Virginal in revealment,
Your bosom's wavering slope,
Concealment,
In fainting heliotrope,
Of whitest white's revealment,

Is like a bed of lilies,
A jealous-guarded row,
Whose will is
Simply chaste dreams: but oh,
The alluring scent of lilies!

Maquillage

The charm of rouge on fragile cheeks,
Pearl-powder, and, about the eyes,
The dark and lustrous eastern dyes;

A voice of violets that speaks
Of perfumed hours of day, and doubtful night
Of alcoves curtained close against the light.

Gracile and creamy white and rose,
Complexioned like the flower of dawn,
Her fleeting colours are as those
That, from an April sky withdrawn,
Fade in a fragrant mist of tears away
When weeping noon leads on the altered day.

Impression

The pink and black of silk and lace,
Flushed in the rosy-golden glow
Of lamplight on her lifted face;
Powder and wig, and pink and lace,

And those pathetic eyes of hers;
But all the London footlights know
The little plaintive smile that stirs
The shadow in those eyes of hers.

Outside, the dreary church-bell tolled,
The London Sunday faded slow;
Ah, what is this? what wings unfold
In this miraculous rose of gold?

On the Heath

Her face's wilful flash and glow
Turned all its light upon my face
One bright delirious moment's space,
And then she passed; I followed slow

Across the heath, and up and round,
And watched the splendid death of day

Upon the summits far away,
And in her fateful beauty found

The fierce wild beauty of the light
That startles twilight on the hills,
And lightens all the mountain rills,
And flames before the feet of night.

At the Cavour

Wine, the red coals, the flaring gas,
Bring out a brighter tone in cheeks
That learn at home before the glass
The flush that eloquently speaks.

The blue-grey smoke of cigarettes
Curls from the lessening ends that glow;
The men are thinking of the bets,
The women of the debts, they owe.

Then their eyes meet, and in their eyes
The accustomed smile comes up to call,
A look half miserably wise,
Half heedlessly ironical.

In the Haymarket

I danced at your ball a year ago,
Tonight I pay for your bread and cheese,
'And a glass of bitter, if you please,
For you drank my best champagne, you know!'

Madcap ever, you laugh the while,
As you drink your bitter and munch your bread;
The face is the same, and the same old smile
Came up at a word I said.

A year ago I danced at your ball,
I sit by your side in the bar tonight;
And the luck has changed, you say that's all!
And the luck will change, you say: all right!

For the men go by, and the rent's to pay,
And you haven't a friend in the world today;
And the money comes and the money goes:
And tonight, who cares! and tomorrow, who knows?

The Absinthe-Drinker

Gently I wave the visible world away.
Far off, I hear a roar, afar yet near,
Far off and strange, a voice is in my ear,
And is the voice my own? the words I say
Fall strangely, like a dream, across the day;
And the dim sunshine is a dream. How clear,
New as the world to lovers' eyes, appear
The men and women passing on their way!

The world is very fair. The hours are all
Linked in a dance of mere forgetfulness.
I am at peace with God and man. O glide,
Sands of the hour-glass that I count not, fall
Serenely: scarce I feel your soft caress,
Rocked on this dreamy and indifferent tide.

Javanese Dancers

Twitched strings, the clang of metal, beaten drums,
Dull, shrill, continuous, disquieting;
And now the stealthy dancer comes
Undulantly with cat-like steps that cling;

Smiling between her painted lids a smile,
Motionless, unintelligible, she twines
Her fingers into mazy lines,
The scarves across her fingers twine the while.

One, two, three, four glide forth, and, to and fro,
Delicately and imperceptibly,
Now swaying gently in a row,
Now interthreading slow and rhythmically,

Still, with fixed eyes, monotonously still,
Mysteriously, with smiles inanimate,
With lingering feet that undulate,
With sinuous fingers, spectral hands that thrill

In measure while the gnats of music whirr,
The little amber-coloured dancers move,
Like painted idols seen to stir
By the idolators in a magic grove.

April Midnight

Side by side through the streets at midnight,
Roaming together,
Through the tumultuous night of London,
In the miraculous April weather.

Roaming together under the gaslight,
Day's work over,
How the Spring calls to us, here in the City,
Calls to the heart from the heart of a lover!

Cool the wind blows, fresh in our faces,
Cleansing, entrancing,
After the heat and the fumes and the footlights,
Where you dance and I watch your dancing.

Good it is to be here together,
Good to be roaming,
Even in London, even at midnight,
Lover-like in a lover's gloaming.

You the dancer and I the dreamer,
Children together,
Wandering lost in the night of London,
In the miraculous April weather.

During Music

The music had the heat of blood,
A passion that no words can reach;
We sat together, and understood
Our own heart's speech.

We had no need of word or sign,
The music spoke for us, and said
All that her eyes could read in mine
Or mine in hers had read.

Tears

O hands that I have held in mine,
That knew my kisses and my tears,
Hands that in other years
Have poured my balm, have poured my wine;

Women, once loved, and always mine,
I call to you across the years,
I bring a gift of tears,
I bring my tears to you as wine.

At Burgos

Miraculous silver-work in stone
Against the blue miraculous skies,

The belfry towers and turrets rise
Out of the arches that enthrone
That airy wonder of the skies.

Softly against the burning sun
The great cathedral spreads its wings;
High up, the lyric belfry sings.
Behold, Ascension Day begun
Under the shadow of those wings!

For a Picture of Watteau

Here, the vague winds have rest;
The forest breathes in sleep,
Lifting a quiet breast;
It is the hour of rest.

How summer glides away!
An autumn pallor blooms
Upon the cheek of day.
Come, lovers, come away!

But here, where dead leaves fall
Upon the grass, what strains,
Languidly musical,
Mournfully rise and fall?

Light loves that woke with spring
This autumn afternoon
Beholds meandering,
Still, to the strains of spring.

Your dancing feet are faint,
Lovers: the air recedes
Into a sighing plaint,
Faint, as your loves are faint.

It is the end, the end,
The dance of love's decease,
Feign no more now, fair friend,
It is the end, the end.

From *London Nights*

Prologue

My life is like a music-hall,
Where, in the impotence of rage,
Chained by enchantment to my stall,
I see myself upon the stage
Dance to amuse a music-hall.

'Tis I that smoke this cigarette,
Lounge here, and laugh for vacancy,
And watch the dancers turn; and yet
It is my very self I see
Across the cloudy cigarette.

My very self that turns and trips,
Painted, pathetically gay,
An empty song upon the lips
In make-believe of holiday:
I, I, this thing that turns and trips!

The light flares in the music-hall,
The light, the sound, that weary us;
Hour follows hour, I count them all,
Lagging, and loud, and riotous:
My life is like a music-hall.

Nora on the Pavement

As Nora on the pavement
Dances, and she entrances the grey hour
Into the laughing circle of her power,

The magic circle of her glances,
As Nora dances on the midnight pavement;

Petulant and bewildered,
Thronging desires and longing looks recur,
And memorably re-incarnate her,
As I remember that old longing,
A footlight fancy, petulant and bewildered;

There where the ballet circles,
See her, but ah! not free her from the race
Of glittering lines that link and interlace;
This colour now, now that, may be her,
In the bright web of those harmonious circles.

But what are these dance-measures,
Leaping and joyous, keeping time alone
With Life's capricious rhythm, and all her own,
Life's rhythm and hers, long sleeping,
That wakes, and knows not why, in these dance-measures

It is the very Nora;
Child, and most blithe, and wild as any elf,
And innocently spendthrift of herself,
And guileless and most unbeguiled,
Herself at last, leaps free the very Nora.

It is the soul of Nora,
Living at last, and giving forth to the night,
Bird-like, the burden of its own delight,
All its desires, and all the joy of living,
In that blithe madness of the soul of Nora.

Violet

This was a sweet white wildwood violet
I found among the painted slips that grow
Where, under hot-house glass, the flowers forget
How the sun shines, and how the cool winds blow.

The violet took the orchid's colouring,
Tricked out its dainty fairness like the rest;
Yet still its breath was as the breath of Spring,
And the wood's heart was wild within its breast.

The orchid mostly is the flower I love,
And violets, the mere violets of the wood,
For all their sweetness, have not power to move
The curiosity that rules my blood.

Yet here, in this spice-laden atmosphere,
Where only nature is a thing unreal,
I found in just a violet, planted here,
The artificial flower of my ideal.

Décor de Théâtre
Behind the Scenes: Empire

The little painted angels flit,
See, down the narrow staircase, where
The pink legs flicker over it!

Blonde, and bewigged, and winged with gold,
The shining creatures of the air
Troop sadly, shivering with cold.

The gusty gaslight shoots a thin
Sharp finger over cheeks and nose
Rouged to the colour of the rose.

All wigs and paint, they hurry in:
Then, bid their radiant moment be
The footlights' immortality!

The Primrose Dance: Tivoli

Skirts like the amber petals of a flower,
A primrose dancing for delight

In some enchantment of a bower
That rose to wizard music in the night;

A rhythmic flower whose petals pirouette
In delicate circles, fain to follow
The vague aerial minuet,
The mazy dancing of the swallow;

A flower's caprice, a bird's command
Of all the airy ways that lie
In light along the wonder-land,
The wonder-haunted loneliness of sky:

So, in the smoke-polluted place,
Where bird or flower might never be,
With glimmering feet, with flower-like face,
She dances at the Tivoli.

La Mélinite: Moulin Rouge

Olivier Metra's Waltz of Roses
Sheds in a rhythmic shower
The very petals of the flower;
And all its roses,
The rouge of petals in a shower.

Down the long hall the dance returning
Rounds the full circle, rounds
The perfect rose of lights and sounds,
The rose returning
Into the circle of its rounds.

Alone, apart, one dancer watches
Her mirrored, morbid grace;
Before the mirror, face to face,
Alone she watches
Her morbid, vague, ambiguous grace.

Before the mirror's dance of shadows
She dances in a dream,
And she and they together seem
A dance of shadows;
Alike the shadows of a dream.

The orange-rosy lamps are trembling
Between the robes that turn;
In ruddy flowers of flame that burn
The lights are trembling:
The shadows and the dancers turn.

And, enigmatically smiling,
In the mysterious night,
She dances for her own delight,
A shadow smiling
Back to a shadow in the night.

Autumn Twilight

The long September evening dies
In mist along the fields and lanes;
Only a few faint stars surprise
The lingering twilight as it wanes.

Night creeps across the darkening vale;
On the horizon tree by tree
Fades into shadowy skies as pale
As moonlight on a shadowy sea.

And, down the mist-enfolded lanes,
Grown pensive now with evening,
See, lingering as the twilight wanes,
Lover with lover wandering.

Colour Studies
At Dieppe

The grey-green stretch of sandy grass,
Indefinitely desolate;

A sea of lead, a sky of slate;
Already autumn in the air, alas!

One stark monotony of stone,
The long hotel, acutely white,
Against the after-sunset light
Withers grey-green, and takes the grass's tone.

Listless and endless it outlies,
And means, to you and me, no more
Than any pebble on the shore,
Or this indifferent moment as it dies.

At Glan-y-Wern

White-robed against the threefold white
Of shutter, glass, and curtains' lace,
She flashed into the evening light
The brilliance of her gipsy face:
I saw the evening in her light.

Clear, from the soft hair to the mouth,
Her ardent face made manifest
The sultry beauty of the South:
Below, a red rose, climbing, pressed
Against the roses of her mouth.

So, in the window's threefold white,
O'ertrailed with foliage like a bower,
She seemed, against the evening light,
Among the flowers herself a flower,
A tiger-lily sheathed in white.

Stella Maris

Why is it I remember yet
You, of all women one has met
In random wayfare, as one meets
The chance romances of the streets,
The Juliet of a night? I know

Your heart holds many a Romeo.
And I, who call to mind your face
In so serene a pausing-place,
Where the bright pure expanse of sea,
The shadowy shore's austerity,
Seem a reproach to you and me,
I too have sought on many a breast
The ecstasy of love's unrest,
I too have had my dreams, and met
(Ah me!) how many a Juliet.
Why is it, then, that I recall
You, neither first nor last of all?
For, surely as I see tonight
The phantom of the lighthouse light,
Against the sky, across the bay,
Fade, and return, and fade away,
So surely do I see your eyes
Out of the empty night arise.
Child, you arise and smile to me
Out of the night, out of the sea,
The Nereid of a moment there,
And is it seaweed in your hair?

O lost and wrecked, how long ago,
Out of the drowning past, I know
You come to call me, come to claim
My share of your delicious shame.
Child, I remember, and can tell
One night we loved each other well,
And one night's love, at least or most,
Is not so small a thing to boast.
You were adorable, and I
Adored you to infinity,
That nuptial night too briefly borne
To the oblivion of morn.
Ah! no oblivion, for I feel
Your lips deliriously steal
Along my neck, and fasten there;

I feel the perfume of your hair,
I feel your breast that heaves and dips,
Desiring my desirous lips,
And that ineffable delight
When souls turn bodies, and unite
In the intolerable, the whole
Rapture of the embodied soul.

That joy was ours, we passed it by;
You have forgotten me, and I
Remember you thus strangely, won
An instant from oblivion.
And I, remembering, would declare
That joy, not shame, is ours to share,
Joy that we had the frank delight
To choose the chances of one night,
Out of vague nights, and days at strife,
So infinitely full of life.
What shall it profit me to know
Your heart holds many a Romeo?
Why should I grieve, though I forget
How many another Juliet?
Let us be glad to have forgot
That roses fade, and loves are not,
As dreams, immortal, though they seem
Almost as real as a dream.
It is for this I see you rise,
A wraith, with starlight in your eyes,
Where calm hours move, for such a mood
Solitude out of solitude;
For this, for this, you come to me
Out of the night, out of the sea.

Hallucination

I

One petal of a blood-red tulip pressed
Between the pages of a Baudelaire:
No more; and I was suddenly aware

Of the white fragrant apple of a breast
On which my lips were pastured; and I knew
That dreaming I remembered an old dream,
Sweeter than any fruit that fruit did seem,
Which, as my hungry teeth devoured it, grew
Ever again, and tantalised my taste.
So, vainly hungering, I seemed to see
Eve and the serpent and the apple-tree,
And Adam in the garden, and God laying waste
Innocent Eden, because man's desire,
Godlike before, now for a woman's sake
Descended through the woman to the snake.
Then as my mouth grew parched, stung as with fire
By that white fragrant apple, once so fair,
That seemed to shrink and spire into a flame,
I cried, and wakened, crying on your name:
One blood-red petal stained the Baudelaire.

II

Is it your face, is it a dream?
Your face I dream in such a mist
Of rosy gold and amethyst?
Is it your eyes that flicker and gleam
Like mocking stars beneath the shade
Of leafy hair that seems to have curled
Its tendrils to blot out the world?
Dreams are the truth: let the world fade!
And these warm spires of heat that rise
Out of my heart into my brain
Are they not flames lighted in vain
At the enchantment of your eyes?
I shudder with the fear of hope,
Giddy expectancy consumes
My senses; but what breath perfumes
The air with scents of heliotrope?
I sicken with a wild desire,
I drown in sweetness, till it seems
As if the after-taste of dreams
Came back into my mouth like fire.

Hands

The little hands too soft and white
To have known more laborious hours
Than those which die upon a night
Of kindling wine and fading flowers;

The little hands that I have kissed,
Finger by finger, to the tips,
And delicately about each wrist
Have set a bracelet with my lips;

Dear soft white little morbid hands,
Mine all one night, with what delight
Shall I recall in other lands,
Dear hands, that you were mine one night!

White Heliotrope

The feverish room and that white bed,
The tumbled skirts upon a chair,
The novel flung half-open, where
Hat, hair-pins, puffs, and paints are spread;

The mirror that has sucked your face
Into its secret deep of deeps,
And there mysteriously keeps
Forgotten memories of grace;

And you half dressed and half awake,
Your slant eyes strangely watching me,
And I, who watch you drowsily,
With eyes that, having slept not, ache;

This (need one dread? nay, dare one hope?)
Will rise, a ghost of memory, if
Ever again my handkerchief
Is scented with White Heliotrope.

Nerves

The modern malady of love is nerves.
Love, once a simple madness, now observes
The stages of his passionate disease,
And is twice sorrowful because he sees,
Inch by inch entering, the fatal knife.
O health of simple minds, give me your life,
And let me, for one midnight, cease to hear
The clock for ever ticking in my ear,
The clock that tells the minutes in my brain.
It is not love, nor love's despair, this pain
That shoots a witless, keener pang across
The simple agony of love and loss.
Nerves, nerves! O folly of a child who dreams
Of heaven, and, waking in the darkness, screams.

Céleste
The Prelude

Child, in those gravely smiling eyes,
What memory sits apart and hears
A litany of low replies,
Love's music, in a lover's ears?

Love in your heart, a guest unsought,
Unfeared, and never known for Love,
Softer than music to the thought,
Sings in an unknown tongue of love.

Song

Her eyes say Yes, her lips say No.
Ah, tell me, Love, when she denies,
Shall I believe the lips or eyes?
Bid eyes no more dissemble,

Or lips too tremble
The way her heart would go!

Love may be vowed by lips, although
Cold truth, in unsurrendering eyes,
The armistice of lips denies.
But can fond eyes dissemble,
Or false lips tremble
To this soft Yes in No?

Clair de Lune

In the moonlit room your face,
Moonlight-coloured, fainting white,
And the silence of the place
Round about us in the night,
And my arms are round about you
In the silence of the night.

Lips that are not mine to kiss,
Lips how often kissed in vain,
Broken seal of memories,
Where the kisses come again
That the lips of all your lovers
Laid upon your lips in vain;

Eyes that are not mine to keep
In the mirror of mine eyes,
Where I tremble lest from sleep
Other ghosts should re-arise;
Why enthrall me with your magic,
Haunting lips, triumphant eyes?

For the silence of the night
Swims around me like a stream,
And your eyes have caught the light
Of a moon-enchanted dream,
And your arms glide round about me,
And I fade into a dream.

Paris

My Paris is a land where twilight days
Merge into violent nights of black and gold;
Where, it may be, the flower of dawn is cold:
Ah, but the gold nights, and the scented ways!

Eyelids of women, little curls of hair,
A little nose curved softly, like a shell,
A red mouth like a wound, a mocking veil:
Phantoms, before the dawn, how phantom-fair!

And every woman with beseeching eyes,
Or with enticing eyes, or amorous,
Offers herself, a rose, and craves of us
A rose's place among our memories.

Bianca: *Presages*

The piteousness of passing things
Haunts her beseeching eyes, the stir
Of those appealing lips, and stings
My senses, hungering for her,
With over-much delight, that brings
A presage of departing things.

I drink the odours of her hair
With lips that linger in her neck,
With lips athirst that wander where
Scarcely the rose of life can fleck
The whiteness of her bosom, bare
Beneath the fragrant veil of hair.

Death in her lilied whiteness lives,
The shadow of Death's eternal lust
After the delicate flesh that gives
The life of lilies to the dust.
Ah, if thy lust my love forgives,
Death, spare this whitest flesh that lives!

Epilogue: Credo

Each, in himself, his hour to be and cease
Endures alone, yet few there be who dare,
Sole with themselves, their single burden bear,
All the long day until the night's release.

Yet, ere the night fall, and the shadows close,
This labour of himself is each man's lot;
All a man hath, yet living, is forgot,
Himself he leaves behind him when he goes.

If he have any valiancy within,
If he have made his life his very own,
If he have loved and laboured, and have known
A strenuous virtue, and a strenuous sin;

Then, being dead, his life was not all vain,
For he has saved what most desire to lose,
And he has chosen what the few must choose,
Since life, once lived, returns no more again.

For of our time we lose so large a part
In serious trifles, and so oft let slip
The wine of every moment, at the lip
Its moment, and the moment of the heart.

We are awake so little on the earth,
And we shall sleep so long, and rise so late,
If there is any knocking at that gate
Which is the gate of death, the gate of birth.

From *Amoris Victima*

Amoris Exsul
Moonrise

I am weary of living, and I long to rest
From the sorrowful and immense fatigue of love;
I have lived and loved with a seeking, passionate zest,
And weariness and defeat are the end thereof.

I have lived in vain, I have loved in vain, I have lost
In the game of Fate, and silently I retire;
I watch the moon rise over the sea, a ghost
Of burning noontides, pallid with spent desire.

In the Forest of Arques

Why am I haunted by your hands?
O subtle and mesmeric palms,
That had the power of what strange calms,
Only my spirit understands;
And you, faint fingers thrilling through
With feverish ecstasies subdued
Into the quiet of your mood,
Why is it that I dream of you?

Exiled and outcast, and resigned
To be forgotten, to forget,
Why is it there should one regret
With one desire possess my mind?
That, in these unfamiliar lands,
After the exile and the change,
You might but soothe me with the strange
Familiar comfort of your hands!

Twilight

The pale grey sea crawls stealthily
Up the pale lilac of the beach;
A bluer grey, the waters reach
To where the horizon ends the sea.

Flushed with a tinge of dusky rose,
The clouds, a twilit lavender,
Flood the low sky, and duskier
The mist comes flooding in, and flows

Into the twilight of the land,
And darkness, coming softly down,
Rustles across the fading sand
And folds its arms about the town.

Arques: Night

The darkness fills the hollows of the moat,
And rises up the valley, and comes down
From the low hills, and wicked white mists float
Like floods about the little town.

The night is all about me, crawling dark
Meshes the doubtful shadows of the way,
And all the woods and all the vales of Arques
Fade as the lamps put out the day.

Then in the darkness, face to face at last
With those winged thoughts that gather to their goal,
I feel their beaks and talons taking fast
Hold on my shivering soul.

Amor Triumphans
The Dance

For the immortal moment of a passionate dance,
Surely our two souls rushed together and were one,
Once, in the beat of our winged feet in unison,
When, in the brief and flaming ardour of your glance,
The world withered away, vanishing into smoke;
The world narrowed about us, and we heard the beat
As of the rushing winds encompassing our feet;
In the blind heart of the winds, eternal silence woke,
And, cast adrift on our unchainable ecstasy,
Once, and once only, heart to heart, and soul to soul,
For an immortal moment we endured the whole
Rapture of intolerable immortality.

From *Images of Good and Evil*

from The Dance of the Daughters of Herodias

They dance, the daughters of Herodias,
Everywhere in the world, and I behold
Their rosy-petalled feet upon the air
Falling and falling in a cadence soft
As thoughts of beauty sleeping. Where they pass,
The wisdom which is wiser than things known,
The beauty which is fairer than things seen,
Dreams which are nearer to eternity
Than that most mortal tumult of the blood
Which wars on itself in loving, droop and die.
But they smile innocently, and dance on,
Having no thought but this unslumbering thought:
'Am I not beautiful? Shall I not be loved?'
Be patient, for they will not understand,
Not till the end of time will they put by
The weaving of slow steps about men's hearts.
They shall be beautiful, they shall be loved.
And though a man's head falls because of them
Whenever they have danced his soul asleep,
It is not well that they should suffer wrong;
For beauty is still beauty, though it slay,
And love is love, although it love to death.

Souls in the Balance
Mater Liliarum

In the remembering hours of night,
When the fierce-hearted winds complain,
The trouble comes into my sight,
And the voices come again,
And the voices come again.

I see the tall white lilies bloom,
(Mother of lilies, pity me!)
The voice of lilies in the room
(Mother of lilies, pity me!)
Crying, crying silently.

The voice of lilies is your voice,
White lily of the world's desire;
And yours, and yours the lily's choice,
To consume whitely, as by fire,
Flawless, flaming, fire in fire.

O lily of the world's despair,
And born to be the world's delight,
Is it enough to have been fair,
To have been pure, to have been white,
As a lily in God's sight?

When the dark hours begin to wake,
And the unslackening winds go by,
There comes a trouble, for your sake:
O is it you, O is it I,
Crying the eternal cry?

I see the phantom lilies wave,
I hear the voices calling me;
O you, that are too pure to save,
Immaculate eternally,
Mother of lilies, pity me!

Opals

My soul is like this cloudy, flaming opal ring.
The fields of earth are in it, green and glimmering,
The waves of the blue sky, night's purple flower of noon,
The vanishing cold scintillations of the moon,
And the red heart that is a flame within a flame.

And as the opal dies, and is reborn the same,
And all the fire that is its life-blood seems to dart
Through the veined variable intricacies of its heart,
And ever wandering ever wanders back again,
So must my swift soul constant to itself remain.
Opal, have I not been as variable as you?
But, cloudy opal flaming green and red and blue,
Are you not ever constant in your varying,
Even as my soul, O captive opal of my ring?

In Ireland
By the Pool at the Third Rosses

I heard the sighing of the reeds
In the grey pool in the green land,
The sea-wind in the long reeds sighing
Between the green hill and the sand.

I heard the sighing of the reeds
Day after day, night after night;
I heard the whirring wild ducks flying,
I saw the sea-gull's wheeling flight.

I heard the sighing of the reeds
Night after night, day after day,
And I forgot old age, and dying,
And youth that loves, and love's decay.

I heard the sighing of the reeds
At noontide and at evening,
And some old dream I had forgotten
I seemed to be remembering.

I hear the sighing of the reeds:
Is it in vain, is it in vain
That some old peace I had forgotten
Is crying to come back again?

In the Wood of Finvara

I have grown tired of sorrow and human tears;
Life is a dream in the night, a fear among fears,
A naked runner lost in a storm of spears.

I have grown tired of rapture and love's desire;
Love is a flaming heart, and its flames aspire
Till they cloud the soul in the smoke of a windy fire.

I would wash the dust of the world in a soft green flood:
Here, between sea and sea, in the fairy wood,
I have found a delicate, wave-green solitude.

Here, in a fairy wood, between sea and sea,
I have heard the song of a fairy bird in a tree,
And the peace that is not in the world has flown to me.

Palm Sunday: Naples

Because it is the day of Palms,
Carry a palm for me,
Carry a palm in Santa Chiara,
And I will watch the sea;
There are no palms in Santa Chiara
Today or any day for me.

I sit and watch the little sail
Lean sideways on the sea,
The sea is blue from here to Sorrento,
And the sea-wind comes to me,
And I see the white clouds lift from Sorrento
And the dark sail lean upon the sea.

I have grown tired of all these things,
And what is left for me?
I have no place in Santa Chiara,

There is no peace upon the sea;
But carry a palm in Santa Chiara,
Carry a palm for me.

The Last Memory

When I am old, and think of the old days,
And warm my hands before a little blaze,
Having forgotten love, hope, fear, desire,
I shall see, smiling out of the pale fire,
One face, mysterious and exquisite;
And I shall gaze, and ponder over it,
Wondering, was it Leonardo wrought
That stealthy ardency, where passionate thought
Burns inward, a revealing flame, and glows
To the last ecstasy, which is repose?
Was it Bronzino, those Borghese eyes?
And, musing thus among my memories,
O unforgotten! you will come to seem,
As pictures do, remembered, some old dream.
And I shall think of you as something strange,
And beautiful, and full of helpless change,
Which I beheld and carried in my heart;
But you, I loved, will have become a part
Of the eternal mystery, and love
Like a dim pain; and I shall bend above
My little fire, and shiver, being cold,
When you are no more young, and I am old.

From *The Loom of Dreams*

The Loom of Dreams

I broider the world upon a loom,
I broider with dreams my tapestry;

58

Here in a little lonely room
I am master of earth and sea,
And the planets come to me.

I broider my life into the frame,
I broider my love, thread upon thread;
The world goes by with its glory and shame,
Crowns are bartered and blood is shed:
I sit and broider my dreams instead.

And the only world is the world of my dreams,
And my weaving the only happiness;
For what is the world but what it seems?
And who knows but that God, beyond our guess,
Sits weaving worlds out of loneliness?

Isolation

When your lips seek my lips they bring
That sorrowful and outcast thing
My heart home from its wandering.

Then, ere your lips have loosed their hold,
I feel my heart's heat growing cold,
And my heart shivers and grows old.

When your lips leave my lips, again
I feel the old doubt and the old pain
Tighten about me like a chain.

After the pain, after the doubt,
A lonely darkness winds about
My soul like death, and shuts you out.

From *The Fool of the World*

Time and Beauty

Your hair, that burning gold
Naked might not behold,

59

Shall tarnish, and your skin
Wrinkle its satin in,
And your lips, like a rose,
Uncolour and unclose;
Yet, because you are made
Of beauty, not arrayed
In beauty's covering,
Hold Time for a vain thing.
Time shall bid youth let fall
Its colours one and all,
And wither in chill air
Bright blood and burning hair;
When these are overpast,
The bones of beauty last.

London

The sun, a fiery orange in the air,
Thins and discolours to a disc of tin,
Until the breathing mist's mouth sucks it in;
And now there is no colour anywhere,
Only the ghost of greyness; vapour fills
The hollows of the streets, and seems to shroud
Gulfs where a noise of multitude is loud
As unseen water falling among hills.
Now the light withers, stricken at the root,
And, in the evil glimpses of the light,
Men as trees walking loom through lanes of night
Hung from the globes of some unnatural fruit.
To live, and to die daily, deaths like these,
Is it to live, while there are winds and seas?

For a Picture of Rossetti

Smoke of battle lifts and lies
Sullen in her smouldering eyes,

Where are seen
Captive bales of merchandise.

Here are shudderings of spears,
Webs of ambush, nets of fears,
Here have been
Prisons, and a place of tears.

In her hair have souls been caught;
Here are snared the strength of thought,
Pride of craft,
Here desire has come to nought.

Have not her lips kissed again
Lips that kissed for love's sake, when
Her lips laughed
Like a passing-bell for men?

This is what Rossetti says
In the crisis of a face.

The Armenian Dancer

O secret and sharp sting
That ends and makes delight,
Come, my limbs call thee, smite
To music every string
Of my limbs quivering.

I strain, and follow on
After a joy in flight,
That flies, and is delight
Only when it is gone,
Not to be looked upon.

I strain, and would embrace
With ardours infinite

61

Some angel of delight
That turns his heavenly face
Ever into void space.

I dance, and as I dance
Desires as fires burn white
To fan the flame delight;
What vague desires advance
With covered countenance?

I dance, and shall not tire
Though music in my sight
Faint before my delight,
And song like a thin fire
Fail before my desire.

The sense within me turns
In labyrinths as of light,
Not dying into delight;
As a flame quickening burns,
Speed in my body yearns.

I stop, a quivering
Wraps me and folds me tight;
I shudder, and touch delight,
The secret and sharp sting,
Suddenly, a grave thing.

The Andante of Snakes

They weave a slow andante as in sleep,
Scaled yellow, swampy black, plague-spotted white;
With blue and lidless eyes at watch they keep
A treachery of silence; infinite

Ancestral angers brood in these dull eyes
Where the long-lineaged venom of the snake

Meditates evil; woven intricacies
Of Oriental arabesque awake,

Unfold, expand, contract, and raise and sway
Swoln heart-shaped heads, flattened as by a heel,
Erect to suck the sunlight from the day,
And stealthily and gradually reveal

Dim cabalistic signs of spots and rings
Among their folds of faded tapestry;
Then these fat, foul, unbreathing, moving things
Droop back to stagnant immobility.

Song of the Sirens

Our breasts are cold, salt are our kisses,
Your blood shall whiten in our sea-blisses;
A man's desire is a flame of fire,
But chill as water is our desire,
Chill as water that sucks in
A drowning man's despairing chin
With a little kissing noise;
And like the water's voice our voice.

Our hands are colder than your lovers',
Colder than pearls that the sea covers;
Are a girl's hands as white as pearls?
Take the hands of the sea-girls,
And come with us to the under-sands;
We will hold in our cold hands
Flaming heart and burning head,
And put thought and love to bed.

We are the last desires; we have waited,
Till, by all things mortal sated,
And by dreams deceived, the scorn
Of every foolish virgin morn,

You, awakening at last,
Drunken, beggared of the past,
In the last lust of despair
Tangle your souls into our hair.

From *Knave of Hearts 1894–1908*

Venice

Water and marble and that silentness
Which is not broken by a wheel or hoof;
A city like a water-lily, less
Seen than reflected, palace wall and roof,
In the unfruitful waters motionless,
Without one living grass's green reproof;
A city without joy or weariness,
Itself beholding, from itself aloof.

Peau d'Espagne

Insinuating monotone,
Why is it that you come to vex,
With your one word, a heart half grown
Forgetful of you, scent of sex?

With that warm overcoming breath
You flow about me like the sea,
And down to some delicious death
Your waves are swift to hurry me.

It is the death of her desire;
The prelude of sleep-heavy sighs,
The pulsing ecstasy of fire,
The wet lips and the closing eyes.

And, Peau d'Espagne, I breathe again,
But, in this ultimate eclipse
Of the world's light, I breathe in vain,
The flower's heart of the unseen lips.

Peau d'Espagne, scent of sex, that brings
To mind those ways wherein I went,
Perhaps I might forget these things
But for that infamy, your scent!

The Tarot Cards

The Tarot cards that rule our fates
Slip through her hands like shaken sands;
Her charmed sight upon them waits,
She holds the future in her hands;
Her fingers can unlatch the gates
That open on forbidden lands.

Under the golden kerchief lies
The mischief of the East; she sees
Beyond our eyesight with her eyes
That are the moons of sorceries;
The soul before them lives and dies
Through countless immortalities.

The shaken cards upon the grass,
Like signs of good and evil things,
Through her obedient fingers pass,
Crowned devils and bright purple kings,
Sad forms in hell, and Sathanas
Rejoicing in his serpent-stings.

Rise up from the accursed pool,
Lest the grass wither where you lie;
Fold up the Tarot cards that rule
Our fates, and put your witchcraft by:
Only a madman or a fool
Would will to know his hour to die.

From *Love's Cruelty*

Studies in Strange Sins (After Beardsley's Designs)
The Woman in the Moon

A naked youth adores the mocking Sun,
With a woman's sidelong eyes and lips,
Before unto the stormless Sea he dips.
The dark girl has the weariness of one
Who, after being satiated, is not won;
He, with some fever in his finger-tips,
Urges the fever in the girl who strips
Her body naked. Sinister, alone,
The dishevelled seaweed shifts under their feet;
Upon the margin of the moonless sea
What shall the end be of their agony?
He to Salome: 'It is the moon we see,
And not the Sun. O moon's maiden, O cheat,
The globe of the Earth, fruit from a fruitless Tree!'

For Des Esseintes
Tragic Dawn

There surged before me the dawn's translucent fires,
For she I loved had left me and I was alone.
In the depths of the midnight I had seen the Unknown.
Astarte was there, the unhated goddess of desires.
And I had seen a spider caught in seven wires
And a gigantic fly no wind had ever blown,
But never to me was the heart of the midnight shown.
The Spirit is never tired but the Soul in me tires.

And in the midst of the flames I was suddenly aware
Of a flame-bird that fluttered on feverish wings
And the night was no longer there nor the night of her hair.
And I was more lonely than God in the heart of things.
When shall the last dawn come with cloudy chariotings?
I shall awake perhaps after that and not find you there.

Translations

From Théophile Gautier

Posthumous Coquetry

Let there be laid, when I am dead
Ere 'neath the coffin-lid I lie,
Upon my cheek a little red,
A little black about the eye.

For I in my close bier would fain,
As on the night his vows were made,
Rose-red eternally remain,
With khol beneath my blue eye laid.

Wind me no shroud of linen down
My body to my feet, but fold
The white folds of my muslin gown
With thirteen flounces, as of old.

This shall go with me where I go:
I wore it when I won his heart;
His first look hallowed it, and so,
For him, I laid the gown apart.

No immortelles, no broidered grace
Of tears upon my cushion be;
Lay me on my own pillow's lace,
My hair across it, like a sea.

That pillow, those mad nights of old,
Has seen our slumbering brows unite,
And 'neath the gondola's black fold
Has counted kisses infinite.

Between my hands of ivory,
Together set for prayer and rest,
Place then the opal rosary
The holy Pope at Rome has blest.

I will lie down then on that bed
And sleep the sleep that shall not cease;
His mouth upon my mouth has said
Pater and *Ave* for my peace.

(*Days and Nights*, 1889)

From Paul Verlaine

Fêtes Galantes
Pantomime

Pierrot, no sentimental swain,
Washes a paté down again
With furtive flagons, white and red.

Cassandre, with demure content,
Greets with a tear of sentiment
His nephew disinherited.

That blackguard of a harlequin
Pirouettes, and plots to win
His columbine that flits and flies.

Columbine dreams, and starts to find
A sad heart sighing in the wind,
And in her heart a voice that sighs.

L'Allée

As in the age of shepherd king and queen,
Painted and frail amid her nodding bows,

Under the sombre branches and between
The green and mossy garden-ways she goes,
With little mincing airs one keeps to pet
A darling and provoking perroquet.
Her long-trained robe is blue, the fan she holds
With fluent fingers girt with heavy rings,
So vaguely hints of vague erotic things
That her eye smiles, musing among its folds.
– Blonde too, a tiny nose, a rosy mouth,
Artful as that sly patch that makes more sly,
In her divine unconscious pride of youth,
The slightly simpering sparkle of the eye.

Fantoches

Scaramouche waves a threatening hand
To Pulcinella, and they stand,
Two shadows, black against the moon.

The old doctor of Bologna pries
For simples with impassive eyes,
And mutters o'er a magic rune.

The while his daughter, scarce half-dressed,
Glides slyly 'neath the trees, in quest
Of her bold pirate lover's sail;

Her pirate from the Spanish main,
Whose passion thrills her in the pain
Of the loud languorous nightingale.

Mandoline

The singers of serenades
Whisper their faded vows
Unto fair listening maids
Under the singing boughs.

Tircis, Aminte, are there,
Clitandre has waited long,
And Damis for many a fair
Tyrant makes many a song.

Their short vests, silken and bright,
Their long pale silken trains,
Their elegance of delight,
Twine soft blue silken chains.

And the mandolines and they,
Faintlier breathing, swoon
Into the rose and grey
Ecstasy of the moon.

(*Silhouettes*, 2nd ed., 1896)

From Stéphane Mallarmé

Sea-Wind

The flesh is sad, alas! and all the books are read.
Flight, only flight! I feel that birds are wild to tread
The floor of unknown foam, and to attain the skies!
Nought, neither ancient gardens mirrored in the eyes,
Shall hold this heart that bathes in waters its delight,
O nights! nor yet my waking lamp, whose lonely light
Shadows the vacant paper, whiteness profits best,
Nor the young wife who rocks her baby on her breast.
I will depart! O steamer, swaying rope and spar,
Lift anchor for exotic lands that lie afar!
A weariness, outworn by cruel hopes, still clings
To the last farewell handkerchief's last beckonings!
And are not these, the masts inviting storms, not these
That an awakening wind bends over wrecking seas,
Lost, not a sail, a sail, a flowering isle, ere long?
But, O my heart, hear thou, hear thou the sailors' song!

(*Images of Good and Evil*, 1899)

Anguish

Tonight I do not come to conquer thee,
O Beast that dost the sins of the whole world bear,
Nor with my kisses' weary misery
Wake a sad tempest in thy wanton hair;
It is that heavy and that dreamless sleep
I ask of the close curtains of thy bed,
Which, after all thy treacheries, folds thee deep,
Who knowest oblivion better than the dead.
For Vice, that gnaws with keener tooth than Time,
Brands me as thee, of barren conquest proud;
But while thou guardest in thy breast of stone
A heart that fears no fang of any crime,
I wander palely, haunted by my shroud,
Fearing to die if I but sleep alone.

(*Poems*, 1902)

Prose

From 'The Decadent Movement in Literature'

The latest movement in European literature has been called by many names, none of them quite exact or comprehensive – Decadence, Symbolism, Impressionism, for instance. It is easy to dispute over words, and we shall find that Verlaine objects to being called a Decadent, Maeterlinck to being called a Symbolist, Huysmans to being called an Impressionist. These terms, as it happens, have been adopted as the badge of little separate cliques, noisy, brainsick young people who haunt the brasseries of the Boulevard Saint-Michel, and exhaust their ingenuities in theorizing over the works they can not write. But, taken frankly as epithets which express their own meaning, both Impressionism and Symbolism convey some notion of that new kind of literature which is perhaps more broadly characterized by the word Decadence. The most representative literature of the day – the writing which appeals to, which has done so much to form, the younger generation – is certainly not classic, nor has it any relation with that old antithesis of the Classic, the Romantic. After a fashion it is no doubt a decadence; it has all the qualities that mark the end of great periods, the qualities that we find in the Greek, the Latin, decadence: an intense self-consciousness, a restless curiosity in research, an over-subtilizing refinement upon refinement, a spiritual and moral perversity. If what we call the classic is indeed the supreme art – those qualities of perfect simplicity, perfect sanity, perfect proportion, the supreme qualities – then this representative literature of today, interesting, beautiful, novel as it is, is really a new and beautiful and interesting disease.

Healthy we can not call it, and healthy it does not wish to be considered. The Goncourts, in their prefaces, in their *Journal*, are always insisting on their own pet malady, *la névrose*. It is in their work too, that Huysmans notes with delight *le style tacheté et faisandé* – high-flavored and spotted with corruption – which he himself

72

possesses in the highest degree. 'Having desire without light, curiosity, without wisdom, seeking God by strange ways, by ways traced by the hands of men; offering rash incense upon the high places to an unknown God, who is the God of darkness' – that is how Ernest Hello, in one of his apocalyptic moments, characterizes the nineteenth century. And this unreason of the soul – of which Hello himself is so curious a victim – this unstable equilibrium, which has overbalanced so many brilliant intelligences into one form or another of spiritual confusion, is but another form of the *maladie fin de siècle*. For its very disease of form, this literature is certainly typical of a civilization grown over-luxurious, over-inquiring, too languid for the relief of action, too uncertain for any emphasis in opinion or in conduct. It reflects all the moods, all the manners, of a sophisticated society; its very artificiality is a way of being true to nature: simplicity, sanity, proportion – the classic qualities – how much do we possess them in our life, our surroundings, that we should look to find them in our literature – so evidently the literature of a decadence?

Taking the word Decadence, then, as most precisely expressing the general sense of the newest movement in literature, we find that the terms Impressionism and Symbolism define correctly enough the two main branches of that movement. Now Impressionist and Symbolist have more in common than either supposes; both are really working on the same hypothesis, applied in different directions. What both seek is not general truth merely, but *la vérité vraie*, the very essence of truth – the truth of appearances to the senses, of the visible world to the eyes that see it; and the truth of spiritual things to the spiritual vision. The Impressionist, in literature as in painting, would flash upon you in a new, sudden way so exact an image of what you have just seen, just as you have seen it, that you may say, as a young American sculptor, a pupil of Rodin, said to me on seeing for the first time a picture of Whistler's, 'Whistler seems to think his picture upon canvas – and there it is!' Or you may find, with Sainte-Beuve, writing of Goncourt, the 'soul of the landscape' – the soul of whatever corner of the visible world has to be realized. The Symbolist, in this new, sudden way, would flash upon you the 'soul' of that which can be apprehended only by the soul – the finer sense of things unseen, the deeper meaning of things evident. And naturally, necessarily, this endeavor after a perfect truth to one's impression, to one's intuition – perhaps an impossible endeavor – has brought with it, in its revolt from ready-made impressions and conclusions, a revolt from the ready-made of language, from the bondage of traditional form, of a form become rigid. In France, where this movement began and has mainly flourished, it is Goncourt who was the first to invent a style in prose really new, impressionistic, a style which was itself almost sensation. It is Verlaine who has invented such another new style in verse. . . .

What the Goncourts have done is to specialize vision, so to speak, and to subtilize language to the point of rendering every detail in just the form and color of the actual impression. Edmond de Goncourt once said to me – varying, if I remember rightly, an expression he had put into the *Journal* – 'My brother and I invented an opera-glass: the young people nowadays are taking it out of our hands.'

An opera-glass – a special, unique way of seeing things – that is what the Goncourts have brought to bear upon the common things about us; and it is here that they have done the 'something new,' here more than anywhere. They have never sought 'to see life steadily, and see it whole:' their vision has always been somewhat feverish, with the diseased sharpness of over-excited nerves. 'We do not hide from ourselves that we have been passionate, nervous creatures, unhealthily impressionable,' confesses the *Journal*. But it is this morbid intensity in seeing and seizing things that has helped to form that marvelous style – 'a style perhaps too ambitious of impossibilities,' as they admit – a style which inherits some of its color from Gautier, some of its fine outline from Flaubert, but which has brought light and shadow into the color, which has softened outline in the magic of atmosphere. With them words are not merely color and sound, they live. That search after *l'image peinte, l'épithète rare*, is not (as with Flaubert) a search after harmony of phrase for its own sake; it is a desperate endeavor to give sensation, to flash the impression of the moment, to preserve the very heat and motion of life. . . .

What Goncourt has done in prose – inventing absolutely a new way of saying things, to correspond with that new way of seeing things which he has found – Verlaine has done in verse. In a famous poem, *Art Poétique*, he has himself defined his own ideal of the poetic art:

> Car nous voulons la Nuance encor,
> Pas la Couleur, rien que la Nuance!
> Oh! la Nuance seule fiance
> Le rêve au rêve et la flûte au cor!

Music first of all and before all, he insists; and then, not color, but *la nuance*, the last fine shade. Poetry is to be something vague, intangible, evanescent, a winged soul in flight 'toward other skies and other loves.' To express the inexpressible he speaks of beautiful eyes behind a veil, of the palpitating sunlight of noon, of the blue swarm of clear stars in a cool autumn sky; and the verse in which he makes this confession of faith has the exquisite troubled beauty – *sans rien en lui qui pèse ou qui pose* – which he commends as the essential quality of verse. In a later poem of poetical counsel he tells us that art should, first of all, be absolutely clear, absolutely sincere: *L'art, mes enfants, c'est d'être absolument soi-même.* The two poems, with their seven years' interval – an interval which means so much in the life of a man like Verlaine – give us all that there is of theory in the work of the least theoretical, the most really instinctive, of poetical innovators. Verlaine's poetry has varied with his life; always in excess – now furiously sensual, now feverishly devout – he has been constant only to himself, to his own self-contradictions. For, with all the violence, turmoil and disorder of a life which is almost the life of a modern Villon, Paul Verlaine has always retained that childlike simplicity, and, in his verse, which has been his confessional, that fine sincerity, of which Villon may be thought to have set the example in literature.

Beginning his career as a Parnassian with the *Poèmes Saturniens*, Verlaine becomes himself, in the *Fêtes Galantes*, caprices after Watteau, followed, a year later, by *La Bonne Chanson*, a happy record of too confident a lover's happiness. *Romances sans Paroles*, in which the poetry of Impressionism reaches its very highest point, is more *tourmenté*, goes deeper, becomes more poignantly personal. It is the poetry of sensation, of evocation: poetry which paints as well as sings, and which paints as Whistler paints, seeming to think the colors and outlines upon the canvas, to think them only, and

75

they are there. The mere magic of words – words which evoke pictures, which recall sensations – can go no further; and in his next book, *Sagesse*, published after seven years' wanderings and sufferings, there is a graver manner of more deeply personal confession – that 'sincerity, and the impression of the moment followed to the letter,' which he has defined in a prose criticism on himself as his main preference in regard to style. . . . To fix the last fine shade, the quintessence of things; to fix it fleetingly; to be a disembodied voice, and yet the voice of a human soul: that is the ideal of Decadence, and it is what Paul Verlaine has achieved. . . .

But to find a new personality, a new way of seeing things, among the young writers who are starting up on every hand, we must turn from Paris to Brussels – to the so-called Belgian Shakespeare, Maurice Maeterlinck.

In truth, Maeterlinck is not a Shakespeare, and the Elizabethan violence of his first play is of the school of Webster and Tourneur rather than of Shakespeare. As a dramatist he has but one note, that of fear; he has but one method, that of repetition.

The window, looking out upon the unseen – an open door, as in *L'Intruse*, through which Death, the intruder, may come invisibly – how typical of the new kind of symbolistic and impressionistic drama which Maeterlinck has invented! I say invented, a little rashly. The real discoverer of this new kind of drama was that strange, inspiring, incomplete man of genius whom Maeterlinck, above all others, delights to honor, Villiers de l'Isle-Adam. Imagine a combination of Swift, of Poe, and of Coleridge, and you will have some idea of the extraordinary, impossible poet and cynic who, after a life of brilliant failure, has left a series of unfinished works in every kind of literature; among the finished achievements one volume of short stories, *Contes Cruels*, which is an absolute masterpiece. Yet, apart from this, it was the misfortune of Villiers never to attain the height of his imaginings, and even *Axël*, the work of a lifetime, is an achievement only half achieved. Only half achieved, or achieved only in the work of others; for, in its mystical intention, its remoteness from any kind of outward reality, *Axël* is undoubtedly the origin of the symbolistic drama. This drama, in Villiers, is of pure symbol, of sheer poetry. It has an exalted eloquence which we find in none of his followers. As Maeterlinck has developed it, it is a drama which appeals directly to the sensations – sometimes crudely, sometimes subtly – playing its variations upon the very nerves themselves. The 'vague spiritual fear' which it creates out of our nervous apprehension is unlike anything that has ever been done before, even by Hoffman, even by Poe. It is an effect of atmosphere – an atmosphere in which outlines change and become mysterious, in which a word quietly uttered makes one start, in which all one's mental activity becomes concentrated on something, one knows not what, something slow, creeping, terrifying, which comes nearer and nearer, an impending nightmare. . . .

But Maeterlinck is by no means anxious to be considered merely or mainly as a dramatist. A brooding poet, a mystic, a contemplative spectator of the comedy of death – that is how he presents himself to us in his work; and the introduction which he has prefixed to his translation of *L'Ornement des Noces Spirituelles*, of Ruysbroeck l'Admirable, shows how deeply he has studied the mystical writers of all ages, and how much akin to theirs is his own temper. Plato and Plotinus, Saint Bernard and Jacob Boehm, Coleridge and Novalis – he knows them all, and it is with a sort of reverence that he sets himself to the task of translating the astonishing Flemish mystic of the thirteenth century, known till now only by the fragments translated into French by Ernest Hello from a sixteenth-century Latin version. This translation and this introduction help to explain the real character of Maeterlinck's dramatic work – dramatic as to form, by a sort of accident, but essentially mystical.

Partly akin to Maeterlinck by race, more completely alien from him in temper than it is possible to express, Joris Karl Huysmans demands a prominent place in any record of the Decadent movement. His work, like that of the Goncourts, is largely determined by the *maladie fin de siècle* – the diseased nerves that, in his case, have given a curious personal quality of pessimism to his outlook on the world, his view of life. Part of his work – *Marthe, Les Sœurs Vatard, En Ménage, A Vau-l'Tau* – is a minute and searching study of the minor discomforts, the commonplace miseries of life, as seen by a peevishly disordered vision, delighting, for its own self-torture, in the insistent contemplation of human stupidity, of the sordid in existence. Yet these books do but lead up to the unique masterpiece, the astonishing caprice of *A Rebours,* in which he has concentrated all that is delicately depraved, all that is beautifully, curiously poisonous, in modern art. *A Rebours* is the history of a typical Decadent – a study, indeed, after a real man, but a study which seizes the type rather that the personality. In the sensations and ideas of Des Esseintes we see the sensations and ideas of the effeminate, over-civilized, deliberately abnormal creature who is the last product of our society: partly the father, partly the offspring, of the perverse art that he adores. Des Esseintes creates for his solace, in the wilderness of a barren and profoundly uncomfortable world, an artificial paradise. His Thébaïde raffinée is furnished elaborately for candle-light, equipped with the pictures, the books, that satisfy his sense of the exquisitely abnormal. He delights in the Latin of Apuleius and Petronius, in the French of Baudelaire, Goncourt, Verlaine, Mallarmé, Villiers; in the pictures of Gustave Moreau, of Odilon Redon. He delights in the beauty of strange, unnatural flowers, in the melodic combination of scents, in the imagined harmonies of the sense of taste. And at last, exhausted by these spiritual and sensory debauches in the delights of the artificial, he is left (as we close the book) with a brief, doubtful choice before him – madness or death, or else a return to nature, to the normal life.

Since *A Rebours*, Huysmans has written one other remarkable book, *Là-Bas*, a study in the hysteria and mystical corruption of contemporary Black Magic. But it is on that one exceptional achievement, *A Rebours*, that his fame will rest; it is there that he has expressed not merely himself, but an epoch. And he has done so in a style which carries the modern experiments upon language to their furthest development. Formed upon Goncourt and Flaubert, it has sought for novelty, *l'image peinte*, the exactitude of color, the forcible precision of epithet, wherever words, images, or epithets are to be found. Barbaric in its profusion, violent in its emphasis, wearying in its splendor, it is – especially in regard to things seen – extraordinarily expressive, with all the shades of a painter's palette. Elaborately and deliberately perverse, it is in its very perversity that Huysman's work – so fascinating, so repellent, so instinctively artificial – comes to represent, as the work of no other writer can be said to do, the main tendencies, the chief results, of the Decadent movement in literature.

(*Dramatis Personae*, Indianapolis, 1923, pp. 96–117)

From 'Dancers and Dancing'

It was in May, 1892, that, having crossed the streets of Paris from the hotel where I was staying, the Hôtel Corneille, in the Latin Quarter (made famous by Balzac in his superb story, *Z. Marcas*), I found myself in Le Jardin de Paris, where I saw for the first time La Mélinite. She danced in a quadrille: young and girlish, the more provocative because she played as a prude, with an assumed modesty; *décolletée* nearly to the waist, in the Oriental fashion. She had long black curls around her face; and had about her a depraved virginity.

And she caused in me, even then, a curious sense of depravity that perhaps comes into the verses I wrote on her. There, certainly, on the night of May 22nd, danced in her feverish, her perverse, her enigmatical beauty, La Mélinite, to her own image in the mirror:

> A shadow smiling
> Back to a shadow in the night

as she cadenced Olivier Métra's *Valse des Roses*.

The *chahut*, which she danced, is the successor, one might almost say the renaissance, of the *cancan*. . . . Of all the stars of the *chahut*, the most charming, the most pleasing, is La Goulue. Still young, though she has been a choreographic celebrity for seven or eight years; still fresh, a veritable 'queen of curds and cream' among the too white and the too red women of the Moulin Rouge; she has that simple, ingenuous air which is, perhaps, the last refinement, to the perverse, of perversity. To dance the *chahut*, to dance it with infinite excitement, and to look like a milkmaid: that, surely, is a triumph of natural genius! Grille-d'Égout, her companion and rival, is not so interesting. She is dark, serious, correct, perfectly accomplished in her art, and a professor of it, but she has not the high spirits, the *entrain*, the attractiveness, of La Goulue. In Nini-Patte-en-l'Air, a later, though an older, leader of the *quadrille naturaliste*, and, like Grille-d'Égout, a teacher of eccentric dancing, we find, perhaps, the most typical representative of the *chahut* of today. She is not young, she is not pretty, she is thin, short of stature, dark, with heavy eyebrows, coarse, irregular features. Her face is worn and haggard, almost ghastly; her mouth is drawn into an acute, ambiguous, ironical smile; her roving eyes have a curious, intent

79

glitter. She has none of the *gaminerie* of La Goulue: hers is a severely self-conscious art, and all her extravagances are perfectly deliberate. But with what mastery they are done, with what tireless agility, what tireless ingenuity in invention! Always cold, collected, 'the Maenad of the Decadence,' it is with a sort of 'learned fury' that she dances; and she has a particular trick – the origin of her nick-name – a particular quiver of the foot as the leg is held rigid in the air – which is her sign and signature. After these three distinguished people come many. There is La Mélinite, Rayon d'Or, La Sauter-elle, Étoile Filante, and many another; of whom La Mélinite is certainly the most interesting. She is tall, slim, boyish in figure, *décolletée* in the Eastern fashion, in a long slit; she dances with a dreamy absorption, a conventional air, as of perverted sanctity, remote, ambiguous. And then there is La Macarona of the Élysée-Montmartre, whose sole title to distinction lies in the extraordinary effrontery of her costume.

(*Colour Studies in Paris*, 1918, pp. 93–7)

'The World as Ballet'

The abstract thinker, to whom the question of practical morality is indifferent, has always loved dancing, as naturally as the moralist has hated it. The Puritan, from his own point of view, is always right, though it suits us, often enough, for wider reasons, to deny his logic. The dance is life, animal life, having its own way passion-ately. Part of that natural madness which men were once wise enough to include in religion, it began with the worship of the disturbing deities, the gods of ecstasy, for whom wantonness, and wine, and all things in which energy passes into an ideal excess, were sacred. It was cast out of religion when religion cast out nature: for, like nature itself, it is a thing of evil to those who renounce instincts. From the first it has mimed the instincts. It can render birth and death, and it is always going over and over the eternal pantomime of love; it can be all the passions, and all the languors; but it idealises these mere acts, gracious or brutal, into more than a picture; for it is more than a beautiful reflection, it has in it life

80

itself, as it shadows life; and it is farther from life than a picture. Humanity, youth, beauty, playing the part of itself, and consciously, in a travesty, more natural than nature, more artificial than art: but we lose ourselves in the boundless bewilderments of its contradictions.

The dance, then, is art because it is doubly nature: and if nature, as we are told, is sinful, it is doubly sinful. A waltz, in a drawing-room, takes us suddenly out of all that convention, away from those guardians of our order who sit around the walls, approvingly, unconsciously; in its winding motion it raises an invisible wall about us, shutting us off from the whole world, in with ourselves; in its fatal rhythm, never either beginning or ending, slow, insinuating, gathering impetus which must be held back, which must rise into the blood, it tells us that life flows even as that, so passionately and so easily and so inevitably; and it is possession and abandonment, the very pattern and symbol of earthly love. Here is nature (to be renounced, to be at least restrained) hurried violently, deliberately, to boiling point. And now look at the dance, on the stage, a mere spectator. Here are all these young bodies, made more alluring by an artificial heightening of whites and reds on the face, displaying, employing, all their natural beauty, themselves full of the sense of joy in motion, or affecting that enjoyment, offered to our eyes like a bouquet of flowers, a bouquet of living flowers, which have all the glitter of artificial ones. As they dance, under the changing lights, so human, so remote, so desirable, so evasive, coming and going to the sound of a thin, heady music which marks the rhythm of their movements like a kind of clinging drapery, they seem to sum up in themselves the appeal of everything in the world that is passing, and coloured, and to be enjoyed; everything that bids us take no thought for the morrow, and dissolve the will into slumber, and give way luxuriously to the delightful present.

How fitly then, in its very essence, does the art of dancing symbolise life; with so faithful a rendering of its actual instincts! And to the abstract thinker, as to the artist, all this really primitive feeling, all this acceptance of the instincts which it idealises, and out of which it makes its own beauty, is precisely what gives dancing its pre-eminence among the more than imitative arts. The artist, it is indeed true, is never quite satisfied with his statue which remains cold, does not come to life. In every art men are pressing forward, more and more eagerly, farther and farther beyond the limits of their art, in the desire to do the impossible: to create life. Realising all humanity to be but a masque of shadows, and this solid world an impromptu stage as temporary as they, it is with a pathetic desire of some last illusion, which shall deceive even ourselves, that we are consumed with this hunger to create, to make something for ourselves, of at least the same shadowy reality as that about us. The art of the ballet awaits us, with its shadowy and real life, its power of letting humanity drift into a rhythm so much of its own, and with ornament so much more generous than its wont.

And something in the particular elegance of the dance, the scenery; the avoidance of emphasis, the evasive, winding turn of things; and, above all, the intellectual as well as sensuous appeal of a living symbol, which can but reach the brain through the eyes, in the visual, concrete, imaginative way; has seemed to make the ballet concentrate in itself a good deal of the modern ideal in matters of artistic expression. Nothing is stated, there is no intrusion of words used for the irrelevant purpose of describing; a world rises before one, the picture lasts only long enough to have been there: and the dancer, with her gesture, all pure symbol, evokes, from her mere beautiful motion, idea, sensation, all that one need ever know of event. There, before you, she exists, in harmonious life; and her rhythm reveals to you the soul of her imagined being.

(*Studies in Seven Arts*, 1906, pp. 387–91)

From *The Symbolist Movement in Literature*

Introduction

The word Symbolism has been used to describe a movement which, during the last generation, has profoundly influenced the course of French literature. All such words, used of anything so living, variable, and irresponsible as literature, are, as symbols themselves must so often be, mere compromises, mere indications. Symbolism, as seen in the writers of our day, would have no value if it were not seen also, under one disguise or another, in every great imaginative writer. What distinguishes the Symbolism of our day from the Symbolism of the past is that it has now become conscious of itself, in a sense in which it was unconscious even in Gérard de Nerval, to whom I trace the particular origin of the literature which I call Symbolist. The forces which mould the thought of men change, or men's resistance to them slackens; with the change of men's thought comes a change of literature, alike in its inmost essence and in its outward form: after the world has starved its soul long enough in the contemplation and the rearrangement of material things, comes the turn of the soul; and with it comes the literature of which I write in this volume, a literature in which the visible world is no longer a reality, and the unseen world no longer a dream. . . .

The interlude, half a mock-interlude, of Decadence, diverted the attention of the critics while something more serious was in preparation. That something more serious has crystallised, for the time, under the form of Symbolism, in which art returns to the one pathway, leading through beautiful things to the eternal beauty.

In most of the writers whom I have dealt with as summing up in themselves all that is best in Symbolism, it will be noticed that the form is very carefully elaborated, and seems to count for at least as much as in those writers of whose over-possession by form I have complained. Here, however, all this elaboration comes from a very different motive, and leads to other ends. There is such a thing as perfecting form that form may be annihilated. All the art of Verlaine is in bringing verse to a bird's song, the art of Mallarmé in bringing verse to the song of an orchestra. In Villiers de l'Isle-Adam drama becomes an embodiment of spiritual forces, in Maeterlinck not even their embodiment, but the remote sound of their voices. It is all an attempt to spiritualise literature, to evade the old bondage of rhetoric, the old bondage of exteriority. Description is banished that beautiful things may be evoked, magically; the regular beat of verse is broken in order that words may fly, upon subtler wings. Mystery is no longer feared, as the great mystery in whose midst we are islanded was feared by those to whom that unknown sea was only a great void. We are coming closer to nature, as we seem to shrink from it with something of horror, disdaining to catalogue the trees of the forest. And as we brush aside the accidents of daily life, in which men and women imagine that they are alone touching reality, we come closer to humanity, to everything in humanity that may have begun before the world and may outlast it.

Here, then, in this revolt against exteriority, against rhetoric, against a materialistic tradition; in this endeavour to disengage the ultimate essence, the soul, of whatever exists and can be realised by the consciousness; in this dutiful waiting upon every symbol by which the soul of things can be made visible; literature, bowed down by so many burdens, may at last attain liberty, and its authentic speech. In attaining this liberty, it accepts a heavier burden; for in speaking to us so intimately, so solemnly, as only religion had hitherto spoken to us, it becomes itself a kind of religion, with all the duties and responsibilities of the sacred ritual.

Conclusion

Allowing ourselves, for the most part, to be but vaguely conscious of that great suspense in which we live, we find our escape from its sterile, annihilating reality in many dreams, in religion, passion, art; each a forgetfulness, each a symbol of creation; religion being the creation of a new heaven, passion the creation of a new earth, and art, in its mingling of heaven and earth, the creation of heaven out of earth. Each is a kind of sublime selfishness, the saint, the lover, and the artist having each an incommunicable ecstasy which he esteems as his ultimate attainment, however, in his lower moments, he may serve God in action, or do the will of his mistress, or minister to men by showing them a little beauty. But it is, before all things, an escape; and the prophets who have redeemed the world, and the artists who have made the world beautiful, and the lovers who have quickened the pulses of the world, have really, whether they knew it or not, been fleeing from the certainty of one thought: that we have, all of us, only our one day; and from the dread of that other thought: that the day, however used, must after all be wasted. . . .

Well, the doctrine of Mysticism, with which all this symbolical literature has so much to do, of which it is all so much the expression, presents us, not with a guide for conduct, not with a plan for our happiness, not with an explanation of any mystery, but with a theory of life which makes us familiar with mystery, and which seems to harmonise those instincts which make for religion, passion, and art, freeing us at once of a great bondage. The final uncertainty remains, but we seem to knock less helplessly at closed doors, coming so much closer to the once terrifying eternity of things about us, as we come to look upon these things as shadows, through which we have our shadowy passage. 'For in the particular acts of human life,' Plotinus tells us, 'it is not the interior soul and the true man, but the exterior shadow of the man alone, which laments and weeps, performing his part on the earth as in a more ample and extended scene, in which many shadows of souls and phantom scenes appear.' And as we realise the identity of a poem, a prayer, or a kiss, in that spiritual universe which we are weaving for ourselves, each out of a thread of the great fabric; as we realise the infinite insignificance of action, its immense distance from the current of life; as we realise the delight of feeling ourselves carried onward by forces which it is our wisdom to obey; it is at least with a certain relief that we turn to an ancient doctrine, so much the more likely to be true because it has so much the air of a dream. On this theory alone does all life become worth living, all art worth making, all worship worth offering. And because it might slay as well as save, because the freedom of its sweet captivity might so easily become deadly to the fool, because that is the hardest path to walk in where you are told only, walk well; it is perhaps the only counsel of perfection which can ever really mean much to the artist.

(*The Symbolist Movement in Literature*, 1899, pp. 5–10, 172–5)

From 'The Choice'

In his escape from the world, one man chooses religion, and seems to find himself; another, choosing love, may seem also to find himself; and may not another, coming to art as to a religion and as to a woman, seem to find himself not less effectually? The one certainty is, that society is the enemy of man, and that formal art is the enemy of the artist. We shall not find ourselves in drawing-rooms or in museums. A man who goes through a day without some fine emotion has wasted his day, whatever he has gained in it. And it is so easy to go through day after day, busily and agreeably, without ever really living for a single instant. Art begins when a man wishes to immortalise the most vivid moment he has ever lived. Life has already, to one not an artist, become art in that moment. And the making of one's life into art is after all the first duty and privilege of every man. It is to escape from material reality into whatever form of ecstasy is our own form of spiritual existence. There is the choice; and our happiness, our 'success in life', will depend on our choosing rightly, each for himself, among the forms in which that choice will come to us.

(*Studies in Prose and Verse*, 1904, pp. 290–1)

From 'A Paradox on Art'

If we may be allowed to look upon art as something essentially independent of its material, however dependent upon its own material each art may be, in a secondary sense, it will scarcely be logical to contend that the motionless and permanent creation of the sculptor in marble is, as art, more perfect than the same sculptor's modelling in snow, which, motionless one moment, melts the next, or than the dancer's harmonious succession of movements which we have not even time to realise individually before one is succeeded by another, and the whole has vanished from before our eyes. Art is the creation of beauty in form, visible or audible, and the artist is the creator of beauty in visible or audible form. But beauty is infinitely various, and as truly beauty in the voice of Sarah Bernhardt or the silence of Duse as in a face painted by Leonardo or a poem written by Blake. A dance, performed faultlessly and by a dancer of temperament, is as beautiful, in its own way, as a performance on the violin by Ysaye or the effect of an orchestra conducted by Richter. In each case the beauty is different, but, once we have really attained beauty, there can be no question of superiority. Beauty is always equally beautiful; the degrees exist only when we have not yet attained beauty.

(*Plays, Acting, and Music*, 2nd ed., 1909, pp. 317–19)

From 'What is Poetry?'

Poetry is first of all an art, and, in art, there must be a complete marriage or interpenetration of substance and form. The writer like Walt Whitman, who seems to contain so much material for poetry, which he can never shape into anything tangibly perfect, is not less disqualified from the name of poet than a writer like Pope, who has the most exquisite control over an unpoetical kind of form which exactly fits an unpoetical kind of substance. Crashaw, who had poetical substance of a particular kind, with only an intermittent power over it, remains a genuine but imperfect poet, whom we must sift with discrimination. Milton, who has almost every quality of form, and many of the finest qualities of substance, becomes the great poet whom he is universally admitted to be, because he is almost always successful in the fusion of substance and form.

(*Studies in Prose and Verse*, 1904, p. 194)

From 'Fact in Literature'

The invention of printing helped to destroy literature. Scribes, and memories not yet spoilt by over-cramming, preserved all the literature that was worth preserving. Books that had to be remembered by heart, or copied with slow, elaborate penmanship, were not thrown away on people who did not want them. They remained in the hands of people of taste. The first book pointed the way to the first newspaper, and a newspaper is a thing meant to be not only forgotten but destroyed. With the deliberate destruction of print, the respect for printed literature vanished, and a single term came to be used for the poem and for the 'news item'. What had once been an art for the few became a trade for the many, and, while in painting, in sculpture, in music, the mere fact of production means, for the most part, an attempt to produce a work of art, the function of written or printed words ceased to be necessarily more than what a Spanish poet has called 'the jabber of the human animal'. Unfortunately, words can convey facts; unfortunately, people in general have an ill-regulated and insatiable appetite for facts. Now music

87

cannot convey facts at all; painting or sculpture can only convey fact through a medium which necessarily transforms it. But literature is tied by that which gives it wings. It can do, in a measure, all that can be done by the other arts, and it can speak where they can but make beautiful and expressive gestures. But it has this danger, that its paint, or clay, or crotchets and quavers, may be taken for the colour, or form, or sound, and not as the ministrants of these things. Literature, in making its beautiful piece of work, has to use words and facts; these words, these facts, are the common property of all the world, to whom they mean no more than what each individually says, before it has come to take on beautiful form through its adjustment in the pattern. So, while paints are of no use to the man who does not understand the science of their employment, nor clay, nor the notations of musical sound, to any but the trained artist, words may be used at will, and no literature follow, only something which many people will greatly prefer, and which they will all have the misfortune to understand. . . .

Facts are difficult of digestion, and should be taken diluted, at infrequent intervals. They suit few constitutions when taken whole, and none when taken indiscriminately. The worship of fact is a wholly modern attitude of mind, and it comes together with a worship of what we call science. True science is a kind of poetry, it is a divination, an imaginative reading of the universe. What we call science is an engine of material progress, it teaches us how to get most quickly to the other end of the world, and how to kill the people there in the most precise and economic manner. The function of this kind of science is to extinguish wonder, whereas the true science deepens our sense of wonder as it enlightens every new tract of the enveloping darkness.

(*Studies in Prose and Verse*, 1904, pp. 1–3)

From 'A Prelude to Life'

I lived in London for five years, and I do not think there was a day during those five years in which I did not find a conscious delight in the mere fact of being in London. When I found myself alone, and in the midst of a crowd, I began to be astonishingly happy. I needed so little, at the beginning of that time. I have never been able to stay long under a roof without restlessness, and I used to go out into the streets, many times a day, for the pleasure of finding myself in the open air and in the streets. I had never cared greatly for the open air in the country, the real open air, because everything in the country, except the sea, bored me; but here, in the 'motley' Strand, among these hurrying people, under the smoky sky, I could walk and yet watch. If there ever was a religion of the eyes, I have devoutly practised that religion. I noted every face that passed me on the pavement; I looked into the omnibuses, the cabs, always with the same eager hope of seeing some beautiful or interesting person, some gracious movement, a delicate expression, which would be gone if I did not catch it as it went. This search without an aim grew to be almost a torture to me; my eyes ached with the effort, but I could not control them. At every moment, I knew, some spectacle awaited them; I grasped at all these sights with the same futile energy as a dog that I once saw standing in an Irish stream, and snapping at the bubbles that ran continually past him on the water. Life ran past me continually, and I tried to make all its bubbles my own.

(*Spiritual Adventures*, 1905, pp. 49–50)

From *London: A Book of Aspects*

In London we have had nothing like the time of Victor Hugo, when Baudelaire and Gautier and Gérard de Nerval and men of obscure and vagabond genius made Paris vital, a part of themselves, a form of creative literature. That is what London has in itself the genius, the men and the material, to be; but of the men of our time only Henley and John Davidson have loved it or struck music out of it.

If we had only had a Walt Whitman for London! Whitman is one of the voices of the earth, and it is only in Whitman that the paving-stones really speak, with a voice as authentic as the voice of the hills. He knew no distinction between what is called the work of nature and what is the work of men. He left out nothing, and what still puzzles us is the blind, loving, embracing way in which he brings crude names and things into his vision, the name of a trade, a street,

89

a territory, no matter what syllables it might carry along with it. He created a vital poetry of cities; it was only a part of what he did; but since Whitman there is no gainsaying it any longer.

When I came to London, I knew nothing of the great things that Whitman had done, or that it was possible to do them in such a way; but I had my own feeling for London, my own point of view there, and I found myself gradually trying to paint, or to set to music, to paint in music, perhaps, those sensations which London awakened in me. I was only trying to render what I saw before me, what I felt, and to make my art out of living material. 'Books made out of books pass away' was a sentence I never forgot, and my application of it was direct and immediate.

I have always been curious of sensations, and above all of those which seemed to lead one into 'artificial paradises' not within everybody's reach. It took me some time to find out that every 'artificial paradise' is within one's own soul, somewhere among one's own dreams, and that haschisch is a poor substitute for the imagination. The mystery of all the intoxicants fascinated me, and drink, which had no personal appeal to me, which indeed brought me no pleasures, found me endlessly observant of its powers, effects, and variations. . . .

I also found a peculiar interest in another part of what is artificial, properly artificial, in London. A city is no part of nature, and one may choose among the many ways in which something peculiar to walls and roofs and artificial lighting, is carried on. All commerce and all industries have their share in taking us further from nature and further from our needs, as they create about us unnatural conditions which are really what develop in us these new, extravagant, really needless needs. And the whole night-world of the stage is, in its way, a part of the very soul of cities. That lighted gulf, before which the footlights are the flaming stars between world and world, shows the city the passions and that beauty which the soul of man in cities is occupied in weeding out of its own fruitful and prepared soil.

That is, the theatres are there to do so, they have no reason for existence if they do not do so; but for the most part they do not do so. The English theatre with its unreal realism and its unimaginative pretences towards poetry left me untouched and unconvinced. I found the beauty, the poetry, that I wanted only in two theatres that were not looked upon as theatres, the Alhambra and the Empire. The ballet seemed to me the subtlest of the visible arts, and dancing a more significant speech than words. I could almost have said seriously, as Verlaine once said in jest, coming away from the Alhambra: 'J'aime Shakespeare, mais . . . j'aime mieux le ballet!' Why is it that one can see a ballet fifty times, always with the same sense of pleasure, while the most absorbing play becomes a little tedious after the third time of seeing? For one thing, because the difference between seeing a play and seeing a ballet is just the difference between reading a book and looking at a picture. One returns to a picture as one returns to nature, for a delight which, being purely of the senses, never tires, never distresses, never varies. To read a book even for the first time, requires a certain effort. The book must indeed be exceptional that can be read three or four times, and no book was ever written that could be read three or four times in succession. A ballet is simply a picture in movement. It is a picture where the imitation of nature is given by nature itself; where the figures of the composition are real, and yet, by a very paradox of travesty, have a delightful, deliberate air of unreality. It is a picture where the colours change, recombine, before one's eyes; where the outlines melt into one another, emerge, and are again lost, in the kaleidoscopic movement of the dance. Here we need tease ourselves with no philosophies, need endeavour to read none of the riddles of existence; may indeed give thanks to be spared for one hour the imbecility of human speech. After the tedium of the theatre, where we are called on to interest ourselves in the improbable fortunes of uninteresting people, how welcome is the relief of a spectacle which professes to be no more than merely beautiful; which gives us, in accomplished dancing, the most beautiful human sight; which provides, in short, the one escape into fairyland which is permitted by that tyranny of the real which is the worst tyranny of modern life. . . .

And there is a charm, which I cannot think wholly imaginary or factitious, in that form of illusion which is known as make-up. To a plain face, it is true, make-up only intensifies plainness; for make-up does but give colour and piquancy to what is already in a face, it adds nothing new. But to a face already charming, how becoming all this is, what a new kind of exciting savour it gives to that real charm! It has, to the remnant of Puritan conscience or consciousness that is the heritage of us all, a certain sense of dangerous wickedness, the delight of forbidden fruit. The very phrase, painted women, has come to have an association of sin, and to have put paint on her cheeks, though for the innocent necessities of her profession, gives to a woman a kind of symbolic corruption. At once she seems to typify the sorceries, and entanglements of what is most deliberately enticing in her sex:

Femina dulce malum, pariter favus atque venenum –

with all that is most subtle, least like nature, in her power to charm. Maquillage, to be attractive, must of course be unnecessary. As a disguise for age or misfortune, it has no interest. But, of all places, on the stage, and, of all people, on the cheeks of young people; there, it seems to me that make-up is intensely fascinating, and its recognition is of the essence of my delight in a stage performance. I do not for a moment want really to believe in what I see before me; to believe that those wigs are hair, that grease-paint a blush; any more than I want really to believe that the actor who has just crossed the stage in his everyday clothes has turned into an actual King when he puts on clothes that look like a King's clothes. I know that a delightful imposition is being practised upon me; that I am to see fairyland for a while; and to me all that glitters shall be gold.

The ballet in particular, but also the whole surprising life of the music halls, took hold of me with the charm of what was least real among the pompous and distressing unrealities of a great city. And some form I suppose of that instinct which has created the gladiatorial shows and the bull-fight made me fascinated by the faultless and fatal art of the acrobat, who sets his life in the wager, and wins the wager by sheer skill, a triumph of fine shades. That love of fine shades took me angrily past the spoken vulgarities of most music-hall singing (how much more priceless do they make the silence of dancing!) to that one great art of fine shades, made up out of speech just lifted into song, which has been revealed to us by Yvette Guilbert.

I remember when I first heard her in Paris, and tried, vainly at the time, to get the English managers to bring her over to London.

She sang 'Sainte Galette', and as I listened to the song I felt a cold shiver run down my back, that shiver which no dramatic art except that of Sarah Bernhardt had ever given me. . . . There was the one great artist of that world which, before I could apprehend it, had to be reflected back to me as in some bewildering mirror. It was out of mere curiosity that I had found my way into that world, into that mirror, but, once there, the thing became material for me. I tried to do in verse something of what Degas had done in painting. I was conscious of transgressing no law of art in taking that scarcely touched material for new uses. Here, at least, was a *décor* which appealed to me, and which seemed to me full of strangeness, beauty, and significance. I still think that there is a poetry in this world of illusion, not less genuine of its kind than that more easily apprehended poetry of a world, so little more real, that poets have mostly turned to. It is part of the poetry of cities, and it waits for us in London.

(*Cities and Sea-Coasts and Islands*, 1918, pp. 198–208)

From 'Impressionistic Writing'

Impressionistic writing requires the union of several qualities; and to possess all these qualities except one, no matter which, is to fail in impressionistic writing. The first thing is to see, and with an eye which sees all, and as if one's only business were to see; and then to write, from a selecting memory, and as if one's only business were to write. It is the interesting heresy of a particular kind of art to seek truth before beauty; but in an impressionistic art concerned, as the art of painting is, with the revelation, the re-creation, of a colored and harmonious world, which (they tell us) owes its very existence to the eyes which see it, truth is a quality which can be attained only by him who seeks beauty before truth. The truth impressionist may be imagined as saying: 'Suppose I wish to give you an impression of the Luxembourg Gardens, as I see them when I look out of my window, will it help to call up in your mind the impression of those glimmering alleys and the naked darkness of the trees, if I begin by telling you that I can count seven cabs, half another at one end, and a horse's head at the other, in the space

93

between the corner of the Odéon and the houses on the opposite side of the street; that there are four trees and three lamp-posts on the pavement; and that I can read the words "Chocolat Menier," in white letters, on a blue ground, upon the circular black kiosk by the side of the second lamp-post? I see those things, no doubt, unconsciously, before my eye travels as far as the railings of the garden; but are they any essential part of my memory of the scene afterward?'

I have turned over page after page of clever, ingenious summarizing of separate detail in a certain book, but I have found nowhere a page of pure beauty; all is broken, jagged, troubled, in this restless search after the broken and jagged outlines of things. It is all little bits of the world seen without atmosphere, and, in spite of many passages which endeavor to draw a moral from clouds, gas, flowers and darkness, seen without sentiment. When the writer describes to us 'the old gold and scarlet of hanging meat; the metallic green of mature cabbages; the wavering russet of piled potatoes; the sharp white of fly-bills, pasted all awry;' we can not doubt that he has seen exactly what he describes, exactly as he describes it, and, to a certain extent, we too see what he describes to us. But he does not, as Huysmans does in the *Croquis Parisiens*, absolutely force the sight of it upon us, so that we see it, perhaps with horror, but in spite of ourselves we see it. Nor does he, when some vague encounter on the road has called up in him a 'sense of the ruthless nullity of life, of the futile deception of effort, of bitter revolt against the extinction of death, a yearning after faith in a vague survival beyond,' convey to us the impression which he has felt in such a way that we, too, feel it, and feel it to be the revelation of the inner meaning of just that landscape, just that significant moment. He has but painted a landscape, set an inexpressive figure in the background, and ticketed the frame with a motto which has nothing to do with the composition.

(*Dramatis Personae*, Indianapolis, 1923, pp. 343–5)

From 'Fantin-Latour and Whistler'

To go from the company of the Fantin-Latours to the company of the Whistlers at the New Gallery is to pass suddenly from a world never quite real into a world as real as day and night. It is a world in which I, for one, find almost everything that I have ever cared to see, or to linger over, in what we call the real world. Here, at least, I see through a painter's vision the world which I have always lived in, a world which is full of beautiful appearances, and which, with all its fullness and satisfaction, is only a shadow and symbol of some supreme beauty, which we can see only through that shadow, but which is assuredly enough for one life. It is Whistler's reality that astonishes me the most, and the variety with which he represents that reality, going clear through outward things to their essence, that is, to their essential reality; never, like Fantin, setting up an invention in the place of nature. It is remarkable that an artist who may seem, in his words, to have denied nature, or to have put himself arrogantly in the place of nature, should, in his pictures have given us no image, no outline, no shade or colour, which is not evoked out of a thing really seen and delicately remembered. . . .

Vulgar curiosity is never gratified in any of Whistler's pictures. He never stared at nature, and you must not stare at his pictures. He treated nature as a gentleman treats a lady, and his fine manners were rewarded by exquisite revelations. I am sure that when he was painting a portrait he tried not to see his sitter, but to let that sitter surprise him, as a delicate artist in words lets himself be surprised by ideas, each surprise being like a sudden light. There is always a certain stealth about magic, and the magical quality did not come into Whistler's pictures by a forthright effort. But he prepared for it, and with ceremony, as one prepares for the reception of a guest.

(*Studies on Modern Painters*, 1925, pp. 32–5)

From 'Aubrey Beardsley'

At times he attains pure beauty, has the unimpaired vision; in the best of the *Salome* designs, here and there afterwards. From the first it is a diabolic beauty, but it is not yet divided against itself. The consciousness of sin is always there, but it is sin first transfigured by beauty, and then disclosed by beauty; sin, conscious of itself, of its inability to escape itself, and showing in its ugliness the law it has broken. His world is a world of phantoms, in whom the desire of the perfecting of mortal sensations, a desire of infinity, has overpassed mortal limits, and poised them, so faint, so quivering, so passionate for flight, in a hopeless and strenuous immobility. They have the sensitiveness of the spirit, and that bodily sensitiveness which wastes their veins and imprisons them in the attitude of their luxurious meditation. They are too thoughtful to be ever really simple, or really absorbed by either flesh or spirit. They have nothing of what is 'healthy' or merely 'animal' in their downward course towards repentance; no overwhelming passion hurries them beyond themselves; they do not capitulate to an open assault of the enemy of souls. It is the soul in them that sins, sorrowfully, without reluctance, inevitably. Their bodies are faint and eager with wantonness; they desire more pleasure than there is in the world, fiercer and more exquisite pains, a more intolerable suspense. They have put off the common burdens of humanity, and put on that loneliness which is the rest of saints and the unrest of those who have sinned with the intellect. They are a little lower than the angels, and they walk between these and the fallen angels, without part or lot in the world.

Here, then, we have a sort of abstract spiritual corruption, revealed in beautiful form; sin transfigured by beauty. And here, even if we go no further, is an art intensely spiritual, an art in which evil purifies itself by its own intensity, and by the beauty which transfigures it. The one thing in the world which is without hope is that mediocrity which is the sluggish content of inert matter. Better be vividly awake to evil than, in mere somnolence, close the very issues and approaches of good and evil. For evil itself, carried to the point of a perverse ecstasy, becomes a kind of good, by means of that energy which, otherwise directed, is virtue; and which can never, no matter how its course may be changed, fail to retain something of its original efficacy. The devil is nearer to God, by the whole height from which he fell, than the average man who has not recognised his own need to rejoice or to repent. And so a profound spiritual corruption, instead of being a more 'immoral' thing than the gross and pestiferous humanity of Hogarth or of Rowlandson, is more nearly, in the final and abstract sense, moral, for it is the triumph of the spirit over the flesh, to no matter what end. It is a form of divine possession, by which the inactive and materialising soul is set in fiery motion, lured from the ground, into at least a certain high liberty. And so we find evil justified of itself, and an art consecrated to the revelation of evil equally justified. . . .

In those drawings of Beardsley which are grotesque rather than beautiful, in which lines begin to grow deformed, the pattern, in which now all the beauty takes refuge, is itself a moral judgement. Look at that drawing called *The Scarlet Pastorale*. In front, a bloated harlequin struts close to the footlights, outside the play, on which he turns his back; beyond sacramental candles have been lighted, and are guttering down in solitude, under an unseen wind. And between, on the sheer darkness of the stage, a bald and plumed Pierrot, holding in his vast, collapsing paunch with a mere rope of roses, shows the cloven foot, while Pierrette points at him in screaming horror, and the fat dancer turns on her toes indifferently. Need we go further to show how much more than Gautier's meaning lies in the old paradox of *Mademoiselle de Maupin*, that 'perfection of line is virtue'? That line which rounds the deformity of the cloven-footed sin, the line itself, is at once the revelation and the condemnation of vice, for it is part of that artistic logic which is morality.

Beardsley is the satirist of an age without convictions, and he can but paint hell as Baudelaire did, without pointing for contrast to any contemporary paradise. He employs the same rhetoric as Baudelaire, a method of emphasis which it is uncritical to think insincere. In that terrible annunciation of evil which he called *The Mysterious Rose-Garden*, the lantern-bearing angel with winged sandals whispers, from among the falling roses, tidings of more than 'pleasant sins'. The leering dwarfs, the 'monkeys', by which the mystics symbolised the earthlier vices; those immense bodies swollen with the lees of pleasure, and those cloaked and masked desires shuddering in gardens and smiling ambiguously at interminable toilets; are part of a symbolism which loses nothing by lack of emphasis. And the peculiar efficacy of this satire is that it is so much the satire of desire returning upon itself, the mockery of desire enjoyed, the mockery of desire denied. It is because he loves beauty that beauty's degradation obsesses him; it is because he is supremely conscious of virtue that vice has power to lay hold upon him. And, unlike those other, acceptable satirists of our day, with whom satire exhausts itself in the rebuke of a drunkard leaning against a lamp-post, or a lady paying the wrong compliment in a drawing-room, he is the satirist of essential things; it is always the soul, and not the body's discontent only, which cries out of these insatiable eyes, that have looked on all their lusts, and out of these bitter mouths, that have eaten the dust of all their sweetnesses, and out of these hands, that have laboured delicately for nothing, and out of these feet, that have run after vanities. They are so sorrowful because they have seen beauty, and because they have departed from the line of beauty.

(*From Toulouse-Lautrec to Rodin*, 1929, pp. 183–7)

From 'Unspiritual Adventures in Paris'

Always, if I can conceive myself under this image, I have lived as a solitary soul lives in the midst of the world. Writing on Walter Pater I said: 'He was quite content that his mind should keep as a solitary prisoner its own dream of the world; it was that prisoner's dream of the world that it was his whole business as a writer to remember to perpetuate.' It is Pater who said of Leonardo da Vinci: 'Yet he is so possessed by his genius that he passes unmoved through the most tragic events, overwhelming his country and friends, like one who comes across them by chance on some secret errand.' As for myself, I have never known what it was to have a home, as most children know it; a home that one has lived in so long that it has got into the ways, the bodily creases, of its inhabitants, like an old, comfortable garment, warmed through and through by the same flesh.

When I think of Baudelaire, and of Verlaine whom I knew, the same sinister sense creeps over me that these, also, were condemned to a kind of perpetual wandering. The artist, it cannot be too clearly understood, has no more part in society than a monk in domestic life: he cannot be judged by its rules, he can be neither praised nor blamed for his acceptance or rejection of its conventions. Social rules are made by normal people for normal people, and the man of genius is fundamentally abnormal.

(*Wanderings*, 1931, p. 77)

98

Fyfield*Books*

Two millennia of essential classics
The extensive Fyfield*Books* list includes

For more information, including a full list of Fyfield*Books* and a contents list for each title, and details of how to order the books in the UK, visit the Fyfield website at www.fyfieldbooks.co.uk or email info@fyfieldbooks.co.uk. For information about Fyfield*Books* available in the United States and Canada, visit the Routledge website at www.routledge-ny.com.